T0278187

IMAGES
*of America*

# HELICOPTER TRAINING
# AT FORT WOLTERS

MINERAL WELLS AND THE VIETNAM WAR

IMAGES
*of America*

# HELICOPTER TRAINING
# AT FORT WOLTERS

MINERAL WELLS AND THE VIETNAM WAR

Wes J. Sheffield

ARCADIA
PUBLISHING

Published by Arcadia Publishing
Charleston, South Carolina

Printed in the United States of America

Library of Congress Control Number: 2024931449

For all general information, please contact Arcadia Publishing:
Telephone 843-853-2070
Fax 843-853-0044
E-mail sales@arcadiapublishing.com

Visit us on the Internet at www.arcadiapublishing.com

*This book is dedicated to all who kept the helicopters flying at Fort Wolters and served our country during the Vietnam War.*

# CONTENTS

Acknowledgments                                         6

Introduction                                            7

1.   The Beginning                                      9

2.   Southern Airways at Wolters                       21

3.   Flight School and Aircraft                        35

4.   International Relations and Students              53

5.   Fort Wolters Community                            63

6.   Vietnam War                                       87

7.   Fort Wolters and Vietnam War Legacy             111

# ACKNOWLEDGMENTS

In 2006, I began writing a narrative history of Vietnam-era Fort Wolters based on interviews with former flight school students and instructors. The majority of the primary sources were Bell Helicopter employees who were also Vietnam veterans and helicopter pilots. During my research, I met Brian Bagnall, a US Army Vietnam veteran and helicopter pilot, whose passion for preserving the history of Fort Wolters turned into a website dedicated to Camp/Fort Wolters history and the Vietnam era. Through Brian, I was introduced to Col. Willie H. Casper Jr. of Mineral Wells, Texas. During the peak years of the Vietnam War, he served as assistant commander of the US Army Primary Helicopter Center at Fort Wolters. While serving at Fort Wolters, Colonel Casper rescued from the trash bin hundreds of Vietnam-era and earlier photographs and written history. The majority of the photographs in this book are from Colonel Casper's collection at the Mineral Wells Library and the National Vietnam War Museum. If not for his diligence in preserving the history of Fort Wolters, these images would be lost in time. I owe a debt of gratitude to both Brian Bagnall and Col. Willie Casper. Both are no longer with us; however, this book is a testament to their love for our country and preserving its military history.

I deeply appreciate the help I received from the following: Mineral Wells Library, Kathy Spencer and Jake Andersen; National Vietnam War Museum, Dr. Jim Messinger, Ean Tillett, and Judy Caldwell; Jim Godfrey; Derek Olson, for sharing photographs for this book; Vietnam Center and Archive director Dr. Steve Maxner and Sheon Montgomery; my son Jake W. Sheffield, for photography and overall tech support; my wife, Cheryl; and my daughter Elyse.

A special thank-you to technical and subject experts and my friends A. Wayne Brown, former Southern Airways flight instructor and chief flight instructor at Bell Helicopter, and Dwayne Williams, Vietnam veteran, decorated combat helicopter pilot, and chief test pilot for Bell Helicopter. Gentlemen, you not only helped create this book, you made the history in it!

# INTRODUCTION

The origins of Fort Wolters began in the 1920s when Mineral Wells was selected as the location for a new permanent Texas National Guard encampment, for the 56th Cavalry Brigade. The new facility was named after the brigade's commanding officer, Texas National Guard brigadier general Jacob F. Wolters. A 50-acre tract of land just outside of the city limits of Mineral Wells was designated as the site of the headquarters of Camp Wolters. Additional acreage was acquired and leased, which expanded the size of Camp Wolters.

In 1939, war erupted in Europe, and it was only a matter of time until the United States would be involved. By June 1940, the German army had steamrolled across central Europe, defeating and occupying Poland, Denmark, Norway, Belgium, the Netherlands, and Luxembourg and forced the surrender of the French government. Great Britain stood virtually alone against the German invasion of Western Europe. US president Franklin Delano Roosevelt urged Congress to increase military funding to prepare the nation. On October 13, 1940, it was announced Mineral Wells was selected as the location for a US Army Infantry Replacement Training Center. The course was set for Mineral Wells, and almost overnight, it transformed from a mineral springs resort to a military town of national significance for the strategy to win World War II.

Construction on Camp Wolters was completed in a record three and one-half months, meeting the March 1, 1941 deadline. During the peak of operation in World War II, Camp Wolters was recognized as the nation's largest Infantry Replacement Training Center, housing 30,000 men at one time. Upon the conclusion of World War II in 1945, military installations across the nation were downsized or closed. Camp Wolters mission was complete. On August 15, 1946, the flag was lowered at Camp Wolters, and it was officially closed. A group of local Mineral Wells investors purchased Camp Wolters from the War Department, and the site was converted into an industrial center known as Camp Wolters Enterprises Inc.

The postwar industrial park at the former Camp Wolters was short-lived. In June 1950, the United States officially entered the Korean War. During the three-year span of the war, US defense spending more than doubled. In late 1950, representatives from the US Air Force and US Army began discussions with company officers of Camp Wolters Enterprises Inc. on the possible use of all of the roads, buildings, and utilities owned by the company. A price was agreed upon, and it was announced in February 1951 that the site was being reactivated and redesignated as Wolters Air Force Base. The newly formed Aviation Engineer Force, SCARWAF (Special Category Army with Air Force), was assigned the mission of training personnel qualified to support aviation construction projects at military installations within the continental limits of the United States and abroad.

In March 1956, Secretary of the Army Wilbur M. Brucker and a group of Defense Department and Army officials arrived at Wolters Air Force Base (AFB) to inspect the facility. The March 24 issue of *Army Times* quoted a source stating orders were issued for Wolters AFB to transfer command and control to the Army, with a mission to provide primary helicopter flight training.

On July 1, 1956, the base was officially transferred to Army control. When the Army regained control of Camp Wolters in 1956, no facilities existed to support the training of helicopter pilots. Construction started in earnest to complete the main heliport, instruction classrooms, four stage fields, and all the necessary access roads on the post. The first class of students in the flight school began in November 1956. During the flight school's first year of operation, the Army awarded a contract to Southern Airways Company, a civilian contractor, to establish and manage a primary flight school and assume responsibility for aircraft maintenance and supporting operations. The civilian Southern Airways instructors conducted the first phase of classroom and in-flight student training, while seasoned military instructors conducted the final phase of flight training, assuring students mastered flying techniques and advanced maneuvers. The school operated two flight training programs—the Officer Rotary Wing Aviator Course (ORWAC), a program specifically for men who had completed Officer Candidate School, and the Warrant Officer Candidate Rotary Wing Aviator Course (WORWAC, commonly referred to as the WOC program). The WOCs were typically men between the ages of 21 to 25 who had already completed basic training and held a rank below that of an officer. Warrant officers were appointed, not commissioned, and received pay close to that of a commissioned officer. In 1963, Camp Wolters was redesignated Fort Wolters to reflect the status of a permanent military installation. In 1966, the post was designated the US Army Primary Helicopter Center.

During the peak Vietnam War years in the late 1960s, approximately 1,300 helicopters would be flying around the Fort Wolters training area air space. The region stretched north toward Jacksboro, south to Stephenville, westward to Breckenridge, and east between Weatherford and Fort Worth. The flight training area encompassed approximately 68,000 square miles. Student pilots were expected to solo within the third to fourth week of flight training. Those who were unsuccessful were "washed out" and eliminated from the flight training program. However, the urgent need for helicopter pilots in Vietnam resulted in closer assessment of student pilot failure rates. Often, students would be recycled through the program to start over. After completing the 16-week course at Fort Wolters, students would complete an additional 16 weeks of advanced flight training at either Fort Rucker in Alabama or Fort Stewart and Hunter Army Airfield in Georgia. After successful completion of primary and advanced flight school, a student aviator was awarded their wings.

In 1967, Fort Wolters's population increased to nearly 10,000 residents, and the helicopter school was graduating 600 students each month. During its 17 years of operation, over 40,000 pilots were trained at Fort Wolters, which included students from South Vietnam and over 33 other US Allied nations. In 1968, newly elected president Richard M. Nixon had campaigned for president promising to achieve an honorable end to the Vietnam War. President Nixon's Vietnamization policies of shifting the responsibility of the war from the United States to the South Vietnamese resulted in the decline of the demand for helicopter pilots. In 1971, the flight school was reduced in size, and the following year, it was announced Fort Wolters would close February 1, 1973. The last class to complete flight school graduated in November 1973. The final closure of Fort Wolters occurred in 1975, and the post once again was converted into an industrial center.

*One*

# THE BEGINNING

Colonel
GAETAM M. ZUCCO
*Commanding Officer*
498th Engr Avn
Brigade

The former World War II US Army Camp Wolters in Mineral Wells, Texas, was reactivated and redesignated Wolters Air Force Base in February 1951. In this 1952 photograph, Col. Gaetan M. Zucco, commander of the 498th Engineer Aviation Brigade, sits proudly at his desk. Wolters AFB was later transferred to US Army control on July 1, 1956. (Courtesy of the National Vietnam War Museum.)

The 498th Engineer Aviation Brigade construction crew in this 1952 photograph is busy making final grade improvements for the completion of a new motor pool area at Wolters AFB. While occupying the base, the 498th constructed new roads, barracks, and a swimming pool and started construction on a new hospital. (Courtesy of the National Vietnam War Museum.)

In this 1952 photograph, airmen are shown standing at retreat at Wolters AFB. The retreat ceremony marks the end of the workday. The US flag is lowered, and service members are required to stand at attention and face the colors of the flag, if visible. If the flag is not within sight, they are to face the direction of the music. (Courtesy of the National Vietnam War Museum.)

Airmen take a refreshment break from a construction project at Wolters AFB in 1952 to visit the mobile exchange truck. Access to the mobile exchange limited downtime on critical projects and allowed work to continue while offering convenience to workers. (Courtesy of the National Vietnam War Museum.)

Upon arriving at Wolters AFB in 1951, the Engineer Aviation Battalion began immediate rehabilitation and construction on base buildings and infrastructure. The former US Army Camp Wolters closed in 1946, and many of the base facilities required repair due to five years of inactivity as a military installation. In this 1951 photograph, contract construction workers are building a new structure. (Courtesy of the National Vietnam War Museum.)

The first aircraft to land at Wolters AFB was a Bell H-13 helicopter in 1951. In this photograph, an airman can be seen on the left guiding the helicopter, while to the right a photographer is kneeling with his camera ready as a group of spectators observe the historic arrival. (Courtesy of the National Vietnam War Museum.)

**First Aircraft to Land at Wolters Air Force Base**

This dedication ceremony program was distributed on July 13, 1956, when Wolters AFB was officially transferred to the US Army. Dedication ceremonies were held at the post in Mineral Wells. Numerous military and local dignitaries attended the ceremony to establish the US Army Primary Helicopter School (USAPHS). (Courtesy of the Willie H. Casper Jr. Collection, Boyce Ditto Public Library.)

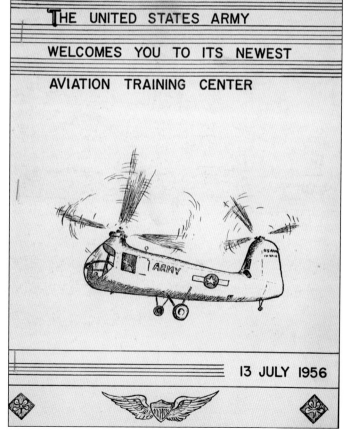

THE UNITED STATES ARMY

WELCOMES YOU TO ITS NEWEST

AVIATION TRAINING CENTER

13 JULY 1956

On July 13, 1956, a portion of the 4th US Army Band performed in the parade during Camp Wolters dedication day ceremonies. In this photograph, military and local dignitaries can be seen in the review stand behind the band. (Courtesy of the Willie H. Casper Jr. Collection, Boyce Ditto Public Library.)

Dignitaries at the Camp Wolters dedication day ceremony are, from left to right, Wilbur M. Brucker, Secretary of the Army Lt. Gen. J.H. Collier, Brig. Gen. John C.B. Elliot, Maj. Gen. William H. Simpson, Maj. Hamilton R. Howze, Camp Wolters commander John L. Inskeep, and Wolters AFB deputy commander Col. Dudley S. Washington. (Courtesy of the Willie H. Casper Jr. Collection, Boyce Ditto Public Library.)

In this dedication day ceremony photograph, Secretary of the Army Wilbur M. Brucker is holding a ceremonial key for the transfer of command of Wolters AFB to the US Army. Standing behind Secretary Brucker are, from left to right, Lt. Gen. J.H. Collier and Brig. Gen. John C.B. Elliot. (Courtesy of the National Vietnam War Museum.)

In this July 13, 1956, photograph, Secretary of the Army Wilbur M. Brucker (left) has a friendly discussion with honor guard leader Col. William N. Beard (right) before the Camp Wolters parade and dedication ceremony in Mineral Wells. (Courtesy of the Willie H. Casper Jr. Collection, Boyce Ditto Public Library.)

In this photograph, Secretary of the Army Wilbur M. Brucker proclaims to those in attendance that Wolters AFB is now under US Army command. Flight training began at Camp Wolters US Army Primary Helicopter School on September 26, 1956. (Courtesy of the Willie H. Casper Jr. Collection, Boyce Ditto Public Library.)

After the parade and Camp Wolters dedication ceremony, a new sign was unveiled at the entrance of the post. In attendance for the unveiling are, from left to right, Col. John L. Inskeep, post commander of Camp Wolters; Lt. Gen. J.H. Collier, Fourth Army commander; and Secretary of the Army Wilbur M. Brucker. (Courtesy of the Willie H. Casper Jr. Collection, Boyce Ditto Public Library.)

In this 1956 Camp Wolters aerial view, a large portion of the land surrounding the Primary Helicopter School Headquarters building is undeveloped. This changed quickly due to the growth and expansion of the flight school. During the school's first year of operation, 250 students completed the program. Ten years later in 1966, the number of students trained increased to over 3,600. (Courtesy of the National Vietnam War Museum.)

In this July 12, 1957, photograph, a Hiller OH-23 Raven helicopter is parked with the engine running in front of the US Army Primary Helicopter School Headquarters. The OH-23 was the initial training helicopter used at the flight school. During its use at Wolters, it logged an impressive 2.5 million flight hours of service. (Courtesy of the National Vietnam War Museum.)

The first class of Camp Wolters primary flight school students graduated on April 27, 1957. In this photograph, Col. Wayne E. Downing, assistant commandant of the school, addresses the graduates. Seated directly behind the right-side microphone in a coat and tie is US congressman Jim Wright of Weatherford, Texas. (Courtesy of the National Vietnam War Museum.)

In this photograph, members of the April 1957 US Army Primary Helicopter School, the first graduating class, stand in formation and proudly display its mascot Mealymouth. The donkey wears a white hard hat and a blanket with the flight school helicopter emblem on its side. (Courtesy of the National Vietnam War Museum.)

During the April 1957 flight school graduation ceremony, Col. William N. Beard (left) extends a handshake to Col. Chester H. Meek (right), Camp Wolters deputy post commander, to confirm acceptance of the operational helicopter facilities constructed by the 931st Engineer Group under his command. (Courtesy of the National Vietnam War Museum.)

Texas governor Price Daniel (left) is holding a model helicopter, while Col. John L. Inskeep (right), Camp Wolters commanding officer, explains a helicopter school display. Governor Daniel was the guest of honor at the March 21, 1958, Mineral Wells Chamber of Commerce dinner at the Baker Hotel. (Courtesy of the National Vietnam War Museum.)

Mrs. Lombardo (left) and her husband, WO Lawrence Lombardo (right), pause at the Camp Wolters welcome sign greeting visitors during the September 1957 one-year anniversary of the flight school. Warrant Officer Lombardo was a graduate of class 57-8 before going to Fort Rucker, Alabama, for advanced flight training. (Courtesy of the National Vietnam War Museum.)

In this November 9, 1956, photograph, Col. John L. Inskeep (left), Camp Wolters commanding officer, observes 1st Lt. Dorothy A. Folmar (right), assistant special services officer, complete the application that designates her as the first Women's Army Corps (WAC) officer member of the Association of the US Army. (Courtesy of the Willie H. Casper Jr. Collection, Boyce Ditto Public Library.)

Col. John L. Inskeep attended the January 15, 1957, ribbon cutting for the grand opening of the Camp Wolters Thrift Shop. In the center of this photograph behind the ribbon, Colonel Inskeep is holding the scissors, while shop manager Mrs. Baird steadies the ribbon. Colonel Inskeep served as the commanding officer and commandant of the US Army Helicopter School from July 1, 1956, until his retirement on July 31, 1961. A graduate of the US Military Academy at West Point in 1931, Inskeep was commissioned a second lieutenant of cavalry upon graduation. During World War II, Inskeep served in Europe and was awarded both the Silver and Bronze Star. Before assuming the duties of the commanding officer of the flight school, Inskeep received his Army aviator wings in May 1956 and was certified as both a fixed-wing and rotary-wing aviator. (Courtesy of the Willie H. Casper Jr. Collection, Boyce Ditto Public Library.)

# Two

# SOUTHERN AIRWAYS AT WOLTERS

Southern Airways Company, a civilian contractor, was awarded a contract in 1956 to establish and manage a primary flight school at Camp Wolters. The center photograph on the cover of this 1960s brochure is the main heliport. It featured parking spaces for 500 helicopters, a maintenance hangar, briefing rooms, a fire station, and a control tower. (Courtesy of the Willie H. Casper Jr. Collection, Boyce Ditto Public Library.)

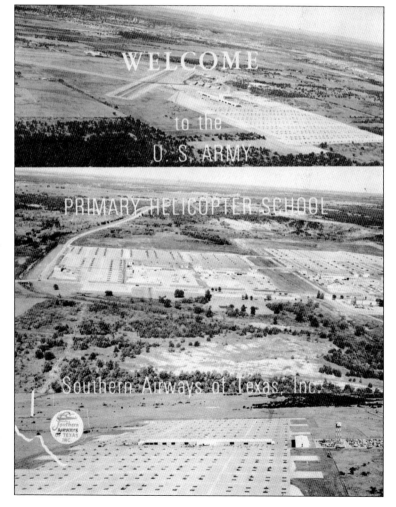

On June 11, 1959, Ramsey Horton, director of materiel at Southern Airways Company, signed a new contract to extend the initial one between the US Army and Southern Airways for another year. Standing from left to right are Maj. John L. Briggs, Larry Hartley, Col. C.H. Meek, and Maj. Brady J. Vradenburg. (Courtesy of the Willie H. Casper Jr. Collection, Boyce Ditto Public Library.)

Southern Airways Company officials posed in front of the Camp Wolters Southern Airways office in this 1957 photograph. From left to right are Dexter K. Nash, seated at the controls of the Hiller OH-23 helicopter; Raymond L. Thomas; and Ramsey Horton. (Courtesy of the Willie H. Casper Jr. Collection, Boyce Ditto Public Library.)

Ramsey Horton (left) of Southern Airways explains operations procedures to Col. John L. Inskeep (second from left) and Brig. Gen. Clifton F. von Kann (third from left), director of Army Aviation. Also pictured in this June 1959 photograph are Raymond L. Thomas (second from right), general manager of Southern Airways, and Maj. John L. Briggs (right), assistant commandant of the USAPHS. (Courtesy of the Willie H. Casper Jr. Collection, Boyce Ditto Public Library.)

Southern Airways employees, dressed in white, observe the May 1962 Best Mess Award presentation. In addition to providing flight training, Southern Airways operated six mess halls, which provided cooks, attendants, and a supervisor for each mess hall. At the beginning of 1968, the mess halls employed over 200 employees, providing over 5,000 meals per day. (Courtesy of the Willie H. Casper Jr. Collection, Boyce Ditto Public Library.)

This May 1958 photograph captures the typical office environment of Camp Wolters civilian Southern Airways employees. Southern Airways administration department had in-house payroll, accounting, and purchasing supply sections supporting the company flight and training operations. The department also managed Southern Airways maintenance, transportation services, and dining facilities. (Courtesy of the National Vietnam War Museum.)

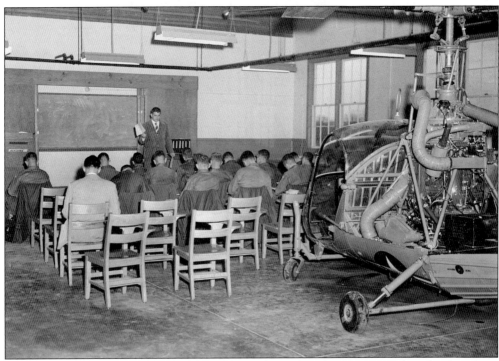

Southern Airways instructor Clifton B. Casler is shown here lecturing to flight school students in a helicopter maintenance class. The group of students in this January 1957 photograph were part of the initial class enrolled in the US Army Primary Helicopter School at Camp Wolters and graduated on April 27, 1957. (Courtesy of the Willie H. Casper Jr. Collection, Boyce Ditto Public Library.)

WOC Joseph L.R. Pinard (right) consults with an unidentified Southern Airways flight instructor during preflight hands-on inspection training. Pinard graduated in the first class at the Camp Wolters US Army Primary Helicopter School, on April 27, 1957. (Courtesy of the Willie H. Casper Jr. Collection, Boyce Ditto Public Library.)

Southern Airways instructor J.M. Kayser is shown in this April 1957 photograph lecturing to senior students in his meteorology class. Several students in the class are wearing squad leader armbands on their uniforms. While in uniform, students were expected to have shined boots at all times. (Courtesy of the Willie H. Casper Jr. Collection, Boyce Ditto Public Library.)

WOC James P. Pickel (first row, right) and other unidentified students listen to a lecture on helicopter maintenance in this April 1957 photograph at Camp Wolters USAPHS. After a noon meal, students were divided into two groups. One group flew helicopters while the others attended classes. Upon completion, the groups would switch to complete the training. (Courtesy of the Willie H. Casper Jr. Collection, Boyce Ditto Public Library.)

A student in Southern Airways instructor Clifton B. Casler's helicopter maintenance course, WOC Joseph L.R. Pinard, points out an important maintenance area on the helicopter. Pinard was the first student in the April 1957 graduating class to fly solo during training. (Courtesy of the Willie H. Casper Jr. Collection, Boyce Ditto Public Library.)

WOC Joseph L.R. Pinard (left) is seated and preparing to fly solo for the first time in a Hiller OH-23D helicopter. Southern Airways instructor Andrew A. Manis (right) gives last-minute instructions and encouragement to his students before liftoff. (Courtesy of the Willie H. Casper Jr. Collection, Boyce Ditto Public Library.)

WOC Joseph L.R. Pinard (left) receives congratulations from Southern Airways instructor Andrew A. Manis (right) after completing the first student solo flight at Camp Wolters USAPHS. Pinard soloed after the minimum of 12 hours of instruction on January 24, 1957. (Courtesy of the Willie H. Casper Jr. Collection, Boyce Ditto Public Library.)

A group of unidentified Southern Airways of Texas employees receive 10-year service pins during a September 25, 1969, ceremony. Southern Airways of Texas Inc. began business operations on February 15, 1964, when it purchased from Southern Airways Company, Atlanta, Georgia, all of its rights and interest in that company's Primary Helicopter Training Division at Fort Wolters. (Courtesy of the Willie H. Casper Jr. Collection, Boyce Ditto Public Library.)

In this September 14, 1970, photograph, two University of Tennessee ROTC graduates, 2nd Lt. Lance D. Workman (in the cockpit) and 2nd Lt. Ronald F. Wolfe, both rotary-wing flight training students, review procedures for the OH-23D helicopter. Tragically, Workman was killed in Vietnam in June 1971 when the helicopter he was copiloting was hit by heavy fire and crashed. (Courtesy of the Willie H. Casper Jr. Collection, Boyce Ditto Public Library.)

Flight student Darrell Folsom (left) checks the logbook of his TH-55A training helicopter as Southern Airways of Texas instructor pilot R.L. Proffitt (right) observes in this November 12, 1971, photograph. The TH-55A was the most widely used helicopter for training at Fort Wolters. (Courtesy of the Willie H. Casper Jr. Collection, Boyce Ditto Public Library.)

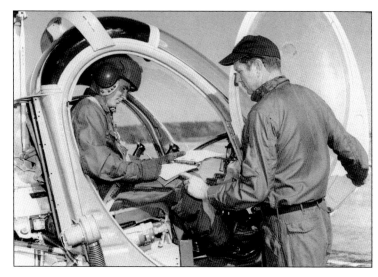

Flight school students, from left to right, 2nd Lt. Douglas Smith (kneeling), WO Johnny Phillips (standing), and 2nd Lt. Darrell Folsom (kneeling) review TH-55A preflight procedures with Southern Airways of Texas instructor R.L. Proffitt (right) in this November 12, 1971, photograph. (Courtesy of the Willie H. Casper Jr. Collection, Boyce Ditto Public Library.)

Southern Airways instructors receiving safety awards during a February 24, 1960, ceremony are, from left to right, (first row) George Fox, Joseph Waller, Deloy Lucas, Allen Mavis, and William Thurmon; (second row) Jimmie Phillips, Porter Hough, Sammy Countryman, Alfred Klotz, and Mauri Sarri; (third row) Ralph MacPherson, Dexter Nash, Richard Case, Leonard MacKenzie, Webb Roberts, and Robert Downs. (Courtesy of the Willie H. Casper Jr. Collection, Boyce Ditto Public Library.)

Southern Airways of Texas flight commander William I. Thurmon (left) and Fred A. Vernon (right), assistant flight commander, were featured in the April 1968 issue of *Southern Views*, the company newsletter. Thurmon has 26 years of flight experience, only exceeded by retired Marine major Vernon, who has 31 years of flight experience. (Courtesy of the Willie H. Casper Jr. Collection, Boyce Ditto Public Library.)

VOLUME 6, NUMBER 9          SEPTEMBER 1971

# FIFTEEN YEARS AT FORT WOLTERS

SOUTHERN AIRWAYS Officials Raymond L. Thomas and Ramsey Horton (deceased) are in front of the aircraft and Dexter K. Nash is at the controls in this 1957 photograph.

Colonel John L. Inskeep (deceased) first Commandant of the Army Primary Helicopter School and Colonel Wayne E. Dowling (deceased) first Assistant Commandant examine an early model of the Hiller.

Other Southern Airways officials in 1957 were L. to R. James E. Leonard, Wayne S. Schwalm, Joseph H. Shields (deceased) and Sam E. Knight.

This month marks the fifteenth anniversary of Southern Airways of Texas, Inc. at Fort Wolters.

Camp Wolters was officially transferred back to the Army on July 1, 1956. The contract to conduct the flight training program at the U. S. Army Primary Helicopter School was awarded August 21, 1956 to Southern Airways Company, a pioneer and leader in the contract flight training field since the first experimental civilian program was conducted in 1940. The Primary Helicopter School became an official U. S. Army School on September 26, 1956. The first class reported for training on November 26, 1956 and graduated April 27, 1957. It consisted of 34 warrant officer candidates and one chief warrant officer. When the Army regained control of Camp Wolters and established the Primary Helicopter School, no facilities existed for training helicopter pilots. The 931st Engineer Group (Construction) was then the primary unit on post and was called upon to construct the main heliport, classrooms, four stagefields and the necessary access roads. From this humble beginning the present facilities have evolved. These include three heliports (one inactive) and 25 stage fields.

The first training fleet consisted of 125 helicopters as compared with over 1300 helicopters in 1969 when the peak was reached.

Total flying time accumulated is in excess of 5 1/3 million hours (at average helicopter speed this would equal over 600 round trips to the moon) and aviation fuel used exceeds 60,000,000 gallons. Many accomplishments, events, and just good times have made their mark in the last fifteen years and this issue of the SOUTHERN VIEWS is dedicated to these. Since one picture is worth a thousand words, pictures will be used to recall the past.

In the September 1971 issue of *Southern Views*, Southern Airways of Texas Inc. published a commemorative collection of stories celebrating 15 years of service at Fort Wolters. Prior to arriving at Fort Wolters, Southern Airways had a rich history of civil aviation training. The company began in 1940 when it was selected to participate in the first experimental Civil Pilot Training Program. In November 1940, the Southern Aviation School was organized for flight training at the Southeast Army Air Force Training Center in Camden, South Carolina. Flight training in PT-17 biplanes began on March 22, 1941. The management of the flight training program at Fort Wolters USAPHS was the largest in Southern Airways company history. During the 17-year span of operations, over 40,000 student pilots were trained, totaling approximately 5.6 million flight hours. (Courtesy of the Willie H. Casper Jr. Collection, Boyce Ditto Public Library.)

During a January 1958 visit to Camp Wolters, this group of touring Southern Airways instructors pause to be briefed by tactical officer 1st Lt. Robert C. Dahn on the responsibilities of the tactical section in the training of helicopter pilots. (Courtesy of the Willie H. Casper Jr. Collection, Boyce Ditto Public Library.)

The Hiller OH-23 was used as a training helicopter at the USAPHS from 1956 until it was transferred out of service in 1971, logging more than 2.5 million training flight hours. In this early-1960s photograph, a Southern Airways maintenance crew performs a scheduled inspection on an OH-23 helicopter. (Courtesy of the National Vietnam War Museum.)

Periodic inspection and maintenance of training helicopters was performed by Southern Airways mechanics. As shown in this photograph, at the end of a day's flying, helicopters were placed in a hangar, uncowled, washed, and inspected for any needed repairs or maintenance. After a positive test flight, the aircraft was approved to return to service. (Courtesy of the National Vietnam War Museum.)

In this early-1960s photograph, Southern Airways mechanics and maintenance crews are busy performing postflight inspection and maintenance on a Hiller OH-23 helicopter. Southern Airways' policy was to provide the maximum availability of aircraft for use by completing maintenance and test flights in one shift to allow for next-day flying. (Courtesy of the National Vietnam War Museum.)

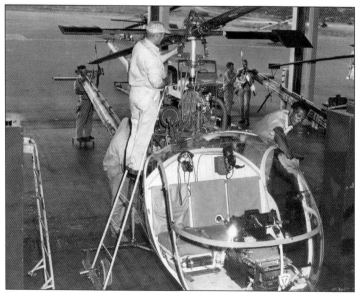

An unidentified Southern Airways mechanic standing on a ladder (left) performs a late afternoon postflight inspection on a Hiller OH-23 rotor hub and yoke while mechanic Charles Brown (right) inspects the mast and transmission in this early-1960s photograph at Camp Wolters USAPHS. (Courtesy of the National Vietnam War Museum.)

On April 13, 1967, a storm hit Downing Heliport at Fort Wolters, and as a result, 179 TH-55 helicopters were damaged. Southern Airways' maintenance department set up an assembly line to rebuild the damaged aircraft. Each helicopter was stripped of components. Airframes were placed in alignment jigs, inspected, repaired, and reassembled. The repair of the 179 helicopters was completed in 90 days. (Courtesy of the Willie H. Casper Jr. Collection, Boyce Ditto Public Library.)

# *Three*

# FLIGHT SCHOOL
# AND AIRCRAFT

A line of new WOCs file into the Fort Wolters US Army Primary Helicopter Center in-processing office. This group of WOCs arrived in 1968 during the peak helicopter pilot training years. The WOCs were typically men between the ages of 21 to 25 who had already completed basic training and held a rank below that of an officer. (Courtesy of the National Vietnam War Museum.)

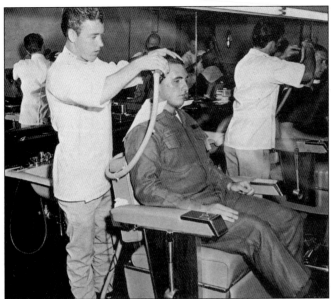

In this 1968 photograph, WOCs receive a regulation induction haircut during in-processing at Fort Wolters US Army Primary Helicopter Center (USAPHC). While historically military induction haircuts were given to prevent the spread of head lice, it also has the psychological purpose of stripping recruits of their individuality and promoting a team mentality. (Courtesy of the National Vietnam War Museum.)

After in-processing at USAPHC, this unidentified WOC becomes familiar with his room in the student barracks. A simple desk, chair, and lamp are available for after-hours study time. Several pairs of shined boots and shoes can be seen under his bunk, which he shares with a fellow student. (Courtesy of the National Vietnam War Museum.)

In the late 1960s, the number of flight school students at Fort Wolters jumped dramatically. The WOC groups jumped from six companies to 10 companies being housed during training. In 1968, the newer brick barracks were full, and the older wooden-style barracks were also used for WOC housing. This barracks also uses several window-unit evaporative coolers. (Courtesy of the National Vietnam War Museum.)

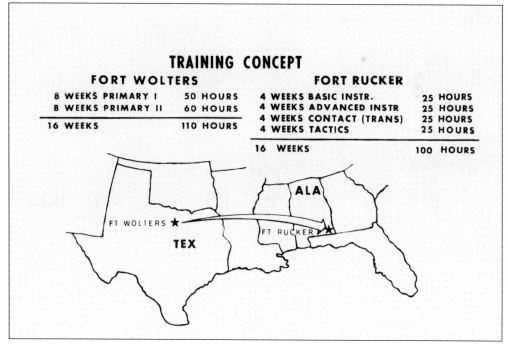

Flight training requirements at Fort Wolters were determined based on the classification of officers or WOC students. Advanced flight training was located at Fort Rucker, Alabama, or Fort Stewart and Hunter Army Airfield, Georgia, not shown on this 1971 training plan graphic. (Courtesy of the National Vietnam War Museum.)

Incoming WOCs at Fort Wolters were required to attend an additional two weeks of preflight training that included military conditioning to learn the responsibilities of a WOC. In this April 11, 1957, photograph, WOC James P. Pickel is crossing the rope line during preflight conditioning training at Camp Wolters USAPHS. (Courtesy of the National Vietnam War Museum.)

In this photograph, WOCs James P. Pickel (first row, left) and Joseph L.R. Pinard (on the immediate right) lead the group while crossing the USAPHS log obstacle confidence course. Preflight training challenged WOCs to achieve top physical condition, which not only prepared them physically, but also mentally to assume the command of a helicopter in combat. (Courtesy of the National Vietnam War Museum.)

In this April 9, 1971, photograph, two unidentified USAPHC WOCs stand at attention as company commander Capt. Robert E. Hess approaches. Before arriving at Fort Wolters, 29-year-old Captain Hess graduated from the University of Maine and was commissioned through the US Army's ROTC program. He completed infantry officer training and earned his wings as a US Army aviator. (Courtesy of the National Vietnam War Museum.)

These three WOCs are starting the day with an early morning breakfast of pancakes and coffee. James P. Pickel (left), Joseph L.R. Pinard (center), and an unidentified man (right) were all members of the first graduating class of April 1957 at Camp Wolters USAPHS. (Courtesy of the Willie H. Casper Jr. Collection, Boyce Ditto Public Library.)

In this November 1970 photograph, a student at Fort Wolters USAPHC undergoes training maneuvers in the Link Trainer. Students received five to six hours of instruction in the Link Trainer during their last two weeks at Fort Wolters to prepare them for instrument training at Fort Rucker, Alabama. The trainer cockpit is that of a TH-13 helicopter. (Courtesy of the Willie H. Casper Jr. Collection, Boyce Ditto Public Library.)

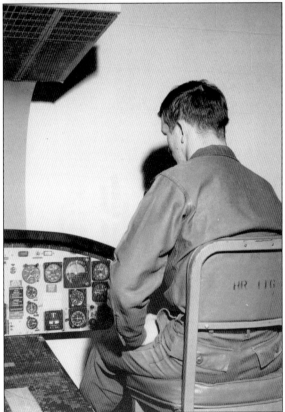

WOC Marshall Karges, a student at Fort Wolters USAPHC, studies a mock-up control panel of a UH-1 helicopter in the school's learning center. Fort Wolters primary flight school graduates, who advanced to Fort Rucker, Alabama, would complete advanced flight training in the Bell UH-1 "Huey," which was the commonly flown helicopter in Vietnam. (Courtesy of the Willie H. Casper Jr. Collection, Boyce Ditto Public Library.)

In this 1971 photograph, WOC Marshall Karges inspects a mock-up of a TH-55 helicopter rotor system. In students' off-duty time, they could examine mock-ups of various systems, view films and slides on helicopter maneuvers and procedures, or study control panels of the TH-55 and UH-1 helicopters. (Courtesy of the Willie H. Casper Jr. Collection, Boyce Ditto Public Library.)

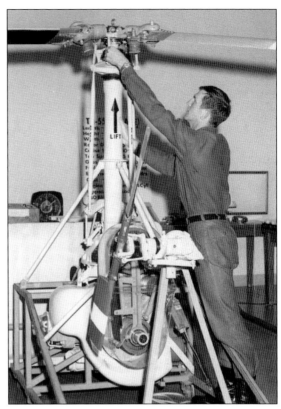

During the Primary I phase of flight training, student pilots were taught basic flight maneuvers of the helicopter at a fixed operation area on a stage field. In this 1969 photograph, two WOCs practice pulling pitch during a simulated flight in a TH-55 helicopter. Phase I training was conducted by civilian Southern Airways of Texas instructors. (Courtesy of the Willie H. Casper Jr. Collection, Boyce Ditto Public Library.)

Second Lt. Joel Randal Woodley, a student at Fort Wolters USAPHC, prepares to take off on a flight training mission in a TH-55 helicopter. Lieutenant Woodley was a 1970 graduate of Stephen F. Austin State University in Nacogdoches, Texas, and received his commission as an infantry officer through the Army's ROTC program. (Courtesy of the Willie H. Casper Jr. Collection, Boyce Ditto Public Library.)

Southern Airways of Texas instructor pilot R.L. Proffitt, observes flight student 2nd Lt. Darrell Folsom as he checks the rotor blades of a TH-55 helicopter during preflight procedures. Students were often given a "TH-55 Cockpit Procedure" card. The laminated card gave instructions on "Before Take Off," "Start Up," and "Shutdown Procedures." (Courtesy of the Willie H. Casper Jr. Collection, Boyce Ditto Public Library.)

In this 1950s photograph, a group of Bell OH-13 helicopters are ready for delivery to Camp Wolters USAPHS. The military version of the Bell 47, the OH-13 was one of the principal helicopters used during the Korean War. It was used at Fort Wolters during the Vietnam War buildup; however, during the 1960s, its use as a trainer was phased out. (Courtesy of the National Vietnam War Museum.)

In this January 1966 photograph, a Hiller OH-23 helicopter is making an approach to land. A three-place aircraft, the OH-23 was used extensively as a primary trainer at Camp/Fort Wolters from 1956 to 1971. It was larger, easier to control, and the preferred helicopter of most students at Fort Wolters USAPHS. (Courtesy of the Willie H. Casper Jr. Collection, Boyce Ditto Public Library.)

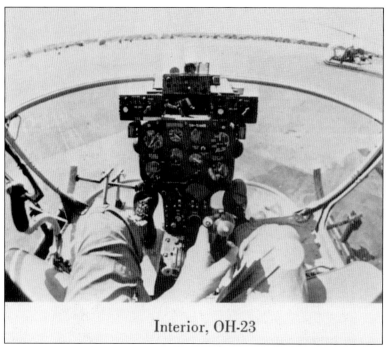

Interior, OH-23

This is an interior cockpit view of the controls for the OH-23 helicopter. The OH-23 was the military version of the Hiller UH-12 helicopter, manufactured by the Hiller Aircraft Company of Palo Alto, California. In addition to serving as a trainer, an armed version was used as an observation helicopter during part of the Vietnam War. (Courtesy of the National Vietnam War Museum.)

The Hughes TH-55A helicopter, shown hovering in this 1969 photograph, was tested in late 1964 and brought into the Fort Wolters USAPHC training fleet in quantity during 1965–1966. The most widely used trainer at Fort Wolters, it reached a total operating fleet of over 760 TH-55 helicopters by the 1970s. (Courtesy of the Willie H. Casper Jr. Collection, Boyce Ditto Public Library.)

The Hughes TH-55A was an off-the-shelf helicopter manufactured by the Hughes Tool Company. As shown in this interior view, it had a compact cockpit and simple controls. The fuselage was steel tube, and two small front wheels on the landing skids added support for ground handling. Smaller in size, flight students referred to the TH-55A as the "Mattel Messerschmidt." (Courtesy of the National Vietnam War Museum.)

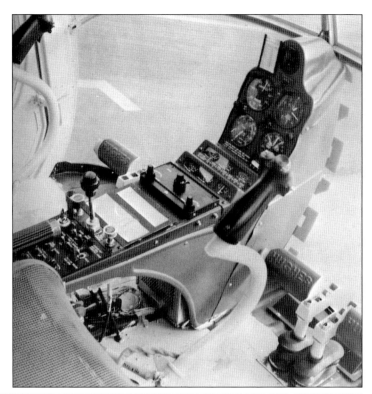

During the Vietnam War, due to the increased demand for helicopter pilots, an additional heliport was constructed to support the USAPHC. Dempsey Heliport was constructed under the supervision of the US Army Corps of Engineers and opened in January 1968. It contained parking spaces for 476 helicopters, a 35,000-square-foot-maintenance hangar, and a control tower. (Courtesy of the Willie H. Casper Jr. Collection, Boyce Ditto Public Library.)

While in the Fort Wolters main heliport tower, Capt. William D. Ray of the USAPHS points out facility features to visitor Harry Frank of Wichita Falls. The main heliport had the capacity to park 500 helicopters. To ensure safety and spacing for aircraft, all helicopter landings and takeoffs were divided into east and west traffic patterns. (Courtesy of the National Vietnam War Museum.)

In this December 10, 1964, photograph, local dignitaries watch a flight demonstration at Stage Field 1, Fort Wolters USAPHS. Stage Field 1, also known as PINTO, had six flight lanes, outside seating for approximately 350, and a permanent control tower. (Courtesy of the Willie H. Casper Jr. Collection, Boyce Ditto Public Library.)

These two Southern Airways flight commanders closely watch their Primary I flight students perform maneuvers at Stage Field 1 at Fort Wolters USAPHC. The flight commander and his assistant serve as tower operators during stage field training. (Courtesy of the Willie H. Casper Jr. Collection, Boyce Ditto Public Library.)

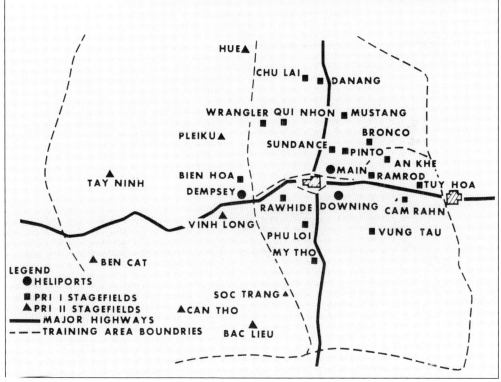

HUE ▲

CHU LAI ■    ■ DANANG

WRANGLER QUI NHON ■ MUSTANG
■    ■

PLEIKU ▲    BRONCO ■
SUNDANCE ■    ■ PINTO

BIEN HOA ■    ● MAIN    ■ AN KHE
■ RAMROD
▲    DEMPSEY ●    ■ TUY HOA
TAY NINH

RAWHIDE DOWNING CAM RAHN
▲
VINH LONG ■    ● VUNG TAU
PHU LOI ■

▲ BEN CAT    MY THO ■

LEGEND
● HELIPORTS
■ PRI I STAGEFIELDS    SOC TRANG ▲
▲ PRI II STAGEFIELDS    ▲ CAN THO
═══ MAJOR HIGHWAYS    ▲
─ ─ ─ TRAINING AREA BOUNDRIES    BAC LIEU

On this 1969 map, the main heliport is shown at its physical location at Fort Wolters. Flight training facilities and stage fields surrounded Fort Wolters from 3 to 36 miles. During the 1960s, many of the stage fields were assigned names of Vietnamese cities. This allowed student pilots to adapt to the use of Vietnamese names during radio communications. (Courtesy of the National Vietnam War Museum.)

Col. Lloyd G. Huggins (left) presents a gate plaque, "A Member of the Team," to Charles Echols (second from left), his son Bill Echols (second from right), and an unidentified man (right). In appreciation of their support of Fort Wolters, private landowners donated free-of-charge access to their property for the construction of stage fields and landing zones used exclusively for flight training. (Courtesy of the National Vietnam War Museum.)

In this undated photograph, a USAPHS flight student practices hovering in a Hiller OH-23 helicopter. During the third to fourth week of flight training, students were expected to fly solo. Students flying solo for the first time were observed by an instructor and their classmates, usually near the end of the training day. (Courtesy of the Willie H. Casper Jr. Collection, Boyce Ditto Public Library.)

In this 1968 photograph, the long-standing tradition at USAPHC of water baptism is being administered to newly soloed student pilots. The ritual was often performed at the Mineral Wells Holiday Inn swimming pool. Before being tossed in, pilots were escorted by their classmates and walked beneath an arched monument of two rotor blades that were permanently placed near the swimming pool. (Courtesy of the National Vietnam War Museum.)

In this May 19, 1960, flight school graduation photograph, honor student 1st Lt. Robert S. Schneider (right) receives his diploma and congratulations from Col. John L. Inskeep (second from right), Camp Wolters USAPHS commander. Also present are Lt. Col. Charles T. Franchina (second from left) and Brig. Gen. William B. Bunker (left), a guest speaker. (Courtesy of the Willie H. Casper Jr. Collection, Boyce Ditto Public Library.)

In this November 30, 1962, photograph, Anne Klieber pins wings on her husband, 2nd Lt. Joseph M. Klieber, during graduation ceremonies. Also pictured is post commander Jack K. Norris. The pinning of wings on primary school graduates was a short-lived practice in the early 1960s. Later, graduates only received their wings after completing advanced training. (Courtesy of the Willie H. Casper Jr. Collection, Boyce Ditto Public Library.)

This April 16, 1959, graduation photograph of Flight-A, Class 59-06 USAPHS, Camp Wolters has both first and second lieutenant officers in the group. Flight school students at Wolters included not only active-duty Army officers, but also warrant officers, enlisted ranks slated to become warrant officers, National Guard officers, officers of Allied countries, and some civilians employed by government agencies. (Courtesy of the National Vietnam War Museum.)

**CLASS 74-08**                                              **2nd W O C COMPANY**
**U. S. ARMY PRIMARY HELICOPTER CENTER--FT. WOLTERS, TEXAS**

This graduation group is one of the last classes to complete primary flight training at Fort Wolters USAPHC. Class 74-07 and class 74-08, totaling 42 students, graduated on November 15, 1973. The graduation ceremony was held in the Fort Wolters Academic Building auditorium. Gen. William J. Maddox Jr., commander of the US Army Aviation Center and commandant of the US Army Aviation School at Fort Rucker, was the guest speaker. After students received their diplomas, General Maddox; Col. Howard M. Moore, Fort Wolters commander and USAPHC commandant; and CSM Willie B. White formally retired the helicopter school colors, officially closing the school and transferring primary helicopter training to Fort Rucker, Alabama. From 1956 to 1973, the US Army Primary Helicopter School at Fort Wolters trained over 40,000 pilots, which included international students from more than 33 foreign countries. (Courtesy of the Willie H. Casper Jr. Collection, Boyce Ditto Public Library.)

After completion of primary flight training at Fort Wolters, pilots then progressed to either Fort Rucker, Alabama, or Fort Stewart and Hunter Army Airfield in Georgia for advanced training in instrument flying, flying in formation, and flying larger aircraft like the Bell UH-1 Huey, which was the helicopter the majority of pilots who were sent to Vietnam flew. The process to complete boot camp, primary flight school at Fort Wolters, and advanced flight training at Fort Rucker took less than one year. In less than a year, a high school graduate could be a warrant officer with 210 hours of flight training and command of a UH-1 helicopter in Vietnam. During the peak training years at Fort Wolters, from the mid-1960s to 1970, the demand for trained helicopter pilots for the Vietnam War spurred growth, leading to the construction of additional heliports and facilities to support a larger student population. (Courtesy of the National Vietnam War Museum.)

# *Four*

# INTERNATIONAL RELATIONS AND STUDENTS

The USAPHS provided flight training to over 30 Allied nations. During the Vietnam War, a large contingent of the South Vietnamese air force trained at Fort Wolters. In this 1963 photograph, three international students enjoy a horseback ride; from left to right are Chadet Nguyen of Vietnam, Syed Tirmizi of Pakistan, and Tran Que Lam of Vietnam. (Courtesy of the Willie H. Casper Jr. Collection, Boyce Ditto Public Library.)

On November 18, 1957, commander of helicopter operations in Algeria for the French army, Lt. Col. Marceau Crestin, toured Camp Wolters USAPHS. Shown are, from left to right, Hiller helicopter company representative Kirby Achee; Colonel Crestin; 2nd Lt. Donald P. Phenix; and Col. John L. Inskeep, Camp Wolters commanding officer. (Courtesy of the National Vietnam War Museum.)

Canadian Army brigadier general Arthur E. Wrinch toured Camp Wolters USAPHS on May 7, 1958. Here, General Wrinch pauses to discuss with Southern Airways director of material Ramsey Horton the maintenance and operational requirements of the US Army helicopters, which are managed under contract by Southern Airways. (Courtesy of the National Vietnam War Museum.)

Maj. Gen. N.H.C. Bray, part of the general staff of the British War Office, London, arrived for a briefing and tour at Camp Wolters USAPHS on February 1, 1957. From left to right are Col. John L. Inskeep, Camp Wolters commanding officer; Major General Bray, and Col. William H. Hyde, aide-de-camp to the general. (Courtesy of the Willie H. Casper Jr. Collection, Boyce Ditto Public Library.)

During his 1957 visit to Camp Wolters, Maj. Gen. N.H.C. Bray examined the Army's OH-23 helicopter. Here, CWO Eldred Bourne points out features of the OH-23 helicopter to General Bray. In the background are, from left to right, Raymond L. Thomas of Southern Airways, J.H. Shields of Southern Airways, and Maj. John L. Briggs of USAPHS. (Courtesy of the Willie H. Casper Jr. Collection, Boyce Ditto Public Library.)

Members of the Greek army visited Camp Wolters on February 27, 1960. Lt. Col. John L. Briggs, assistant commandant, USAPHS, explains methods of approach for landing at a stage field. From left to right are Lt. Col. Alan B. Abt, interpreter; Gen. Georgies Beneoukas; Col. Odysseus M. Angelis; Maj. Anististidis Vlahous, and Col. Dimetrios G. Andriotis. (Courtesy of the Willie H. Casper Jr. Collection, Boyce Ditto Public Library.)

Honor graduate Maj. Susumu Yamasaki of the Japanese army receives his diploma from Col. John L. Inskeep, Camp Wolters commander at the USAPHS class graduation on May 20, 1960. Present to extend their congratulations to Major Yamasaki are, from left to right, Raymond Thomas, general manager of Southern Airways, and Brig. Gen. Williams B. Bunker, guest speaker. (Courtesy of the Willie H. Casper Jr. Collection, Boyce Ditto Public Library.)

Maj. Joseph Stangl of the Austrian army air corps toured Camp Wolters USAPHS on September 6, 1960. Southern Airways flight instructor Heinz Zeiger (left) served as both tour guide and interpreter. Zeiger is shown here discussing the features of the OH-23 helicopter with Major Stangl. (Courtesy of the National Vietnam War Museum.)

Southern Airways director of maintenance Wayne Schwalm smiles for the camera while acting as a tour guide for five Republic of Korea Army Aviation officers. The officers toured the Southern Airways facility at Camp Wolters on February 6, 1961. From left to right are Lt. Col. Dongjun Lee, Lt. Col. Songchohl Pak, Schwalm, Col. Yohngul Son, Lt. Col. Chijik Ke, and Lt. Duksoon Pak. (Courtesy of the National Vietnam War Museum.)

Air Commodore H.A.C. Bird-Wilson of the British Royal Air Force and five other British officers were given a tour of a ranch near Fort Wolters during their December 12, 1964, visit. Commodore Bird-Wilson is shown here trying on a pair of chaps. Assisting are Col. Kemuel K. Blacker (left), Fort Wolters commander and USAPHS commandant, and Charles Lee (right), landowner. (Courtesy of the National Vietnam War Museum.)

At the July 6, 1965, Mineral Wells Chamber of Commerce meeting, honorary membership was presented to this group of Vietnamese cadets attending USAPHS. Shown from left to right are Cpt. Arthur Dimsdale, USAPHS; Marshall Hamilton, Mineral Wells Chamber of Commerce; Nguyen Kinh Hiep; Nguyen Quang Thai; Perry Horton; Vu Ngoc Nguyen; Le Huu Duc; Nguyen Van Lap; and an unidentified man. (Courtesy of the Willie H. Casper Jr. Collection, Boyce Ditto Public Library.)

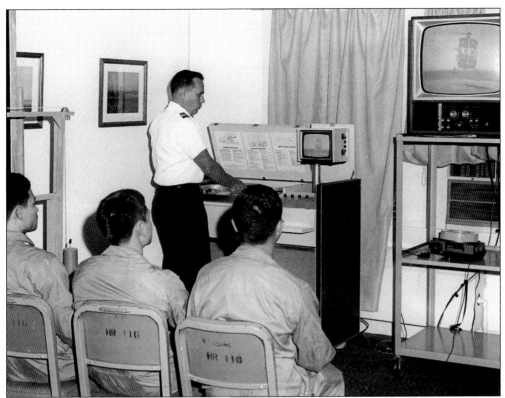

In this 1969 photograph, members of the Vietnam -Air Force view televised flight procedure instructions that were produced in-house at Fort Wolters by the USAPHS Training Support Department. The Educational Television Branch of the Training Support Department produced television tapes for training and operated six closed-circuit television channels. (Courtesy of the Willie H. Casper Jr. Collection, Boyce Ditto Public Library.)

Two unidentified Vietnam Air Force flight students observe the operation of a flight balance training device in the USAPHS Learning Center. All flight students had access to the Learning Center, which was open during regular duty and after hours. Films, tape recordings, reference materials, and unique training devices were available to sharpen student skills and understanding. (Courtesy of the Willie H. Casper Jr. Collection, Boyce Ditto Public Library.)

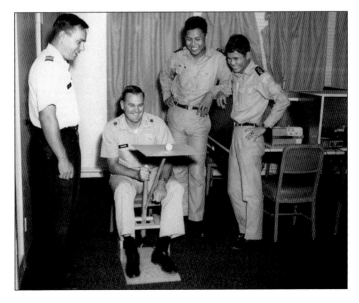

In this 1969 photograph, two unidentified Vietnam Air Force flight students select items from the Vietnamese lunch menu. From 1968 to 1970, a large number of Vietnamese students were attending flight school at Fort Wolters. Southern Airways, which managed the dining facilities, opened a dining hall that served only authentic Vietnamese food. (Courtesy of the Willie H. Casper Jr. Collection, Boyce Ditto Public Library.)

Lieu Thi Franke (center), a native of Vietnam, sees that authentic Vietnamese food is served to international students attending USAPHS. From 1968 through 1970, Southern Airways operated seven dining halls at Fort Wolters, serving in excess of 12,000 meals per day. (Courtesy of the Willie H. Casper Jr. Collection, Boyce Ditto Public Library.)

While visiting the Fort Wolters Post Exchange on November 10, 1971, Vietnam Air Force flight school student Wo Tay seems interested in purchasing *The Yes Album*. Shopping at the post exchange was a convenient close option for international students attending flight school. (Courtesy of the Willie H. Casper Jr. Collection, Boyce Ditto Public Library.)

Second Lt. Joel Randal Woodley, a 1970 graduate of Stephen F. Austin State University and new student at USAPHS, introduces his wife, Martha Faye, to his unidentified Vietnam Air Force classmates while on a shopping trip to the Fort Wolters Post Exchange. (Courtesy of the Willie H. Casper Jr. Collection, Boyce Ditto Public Library.)

In this June 5, 1961, photograph, two Allied USAPHS students training with the Officer Rotary Wing Aviator Course, Class 11-A, discuss a just completed training flight in an OH-23 helicopter at Camp Wolters main heliport. From left to right are Capt. Myint Win from Rangoon Burma and 2nd Lt. Chit Tin from Maymyo, Burma. International students attending USAPHS classes trained and comingled with other US military students. In addition to cockpit flight training, coursework included maintenance, aerodynamics, flying safety, navigation, weather training, and radio communications. The South Vietnamese Air Force students were the largest international student population trained at Fort Wolters, to support the demand for helicopter pilots for the Vietnam War. In addition to Vietnam, students from the following countries were trained at USAPHS: Australia, Great Britain, Burma, Chili, France, Germany, Guatemala, Indonesia, Iran, Italy, Laos, Malaysia, Mexico, Pakistan, Peru, and Turkey. (Courtesy of the National Vietnam War Museum.)

*Five*

# FORT WOLTERS
# COMMUNITY

This group of Girl Scouts is assembled at Fort Wolters post headquarters to observe Girl Scout Week, March 7–13, 1965. Girls Scout Week is celebrated each March, starting with Girl Scout Sunday and ending with Girl Scout Sabbath on a Saturday. The group stands at attention for retreat, the end of the workday, to secure and pay respect to the American flag. (Courtesy of the National Vietnam War Museum.)

The 697th Engineer Company softball team was the winner of the 1963 Fort Wolters championship. The company commander for the team is Capt. James Hoefener (third row, far right). Team sports among post companies were popular and often well-attended rivalry events. (Courtesy of the National Vietnam War Museum.)

The Camp Wolters basketball team, pictured in February 1957, advanced to the Fourth Army Tournament at Fort Sill, Oklahoma. Team members are, from left to right, (first row) Harry J. Miller (equipment manager), Willie A. Miller, Ronald M. Manaker, Alfred Money, Gerald Dammann, Arnold Pease, and Gail F. Huddleston; (second row) Clarence Riley, Jimmie Downing, Robert Graben, Wade Blankenship, and Fritz Dorner. (Courtesy of the Willie H. Casper Jr. Collection, Boyce Ditto Public Library.)

In February 1957, the Camp Wolters bowling team competed in the Fourth Army Tournament at Fort Sam Houston, Texas. Team members are, from left to right, Alan Baird, David Holbrook, Larry Muir, Ronald Stoops, James Zuelzke, Albert Niemic, Frank Houge, and William Hargrave. (Courtesy of the Willie H. Casper Jr. Collection, Boyce Ditto Public Library.)

In this July 18, 1962, photograph, a Camp Wolters competition bowler, US Army specialist J.E. Paine of the 864th Engineer Battalion, proudly displays his third place trophy, won at the World Wide Corp of Engineer Bowling Tournament. (Courtesy of the Willie H. Casper Jr. Collection, Boyce Ditto Public Library.)

The Camp Wolters small-bore rifle team participated in the 1962 Fourth US Army Postal Match. Members are, from left to right, (first row) Dan Hernandez, Charles R. Endsley, William Stitt, William L. Goss, and Dick Kemp; (second row) George Reneau, Larry A. Schuller, John O. Neely, James P. Starrett, and Joel A. Peterson. (Courtesy of the Willie H. Casper Jr. Collection, Boyce Ditto Public Library.)

These two Camp Wolters Girl Scouts believe in starting at the top. Dena Cipolla (left) and Rachel Ann Rajchel (right) sell their first box to Col. John L. Inskeep during the 1957 cookie drive. The proceeds of the sale further the Girl Scouts' mission of service to home, community, and nation. (Courtesy of the Willie H. Casper Jr. Collection, Boyce Ditto Public Library.)

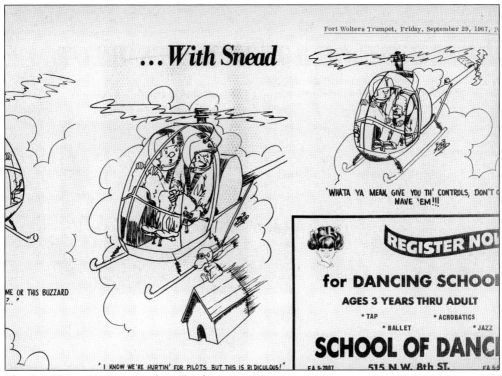

... With Snead

"WHATA YA MEAN, GIVE YOU TH' CONTROLS, DON'T
HAVE 'EM!!!"

ME OR THIS BUZZARD
?.."

" I KNOW WE'RE HURTIN' FOR PILOTS BUT THIS IS RIDICULOUS!"

The *Fort Wolters Trumpet* was the official newspaper for Fort Wolters. In this September 29, 1967, issue, several of WO George Robert "Bob" Snead's hand-drawn cartoons were published. A self-taught cartoonist and artist, Snead had a regular cartoon feature for three years in *Army Times* magazine entitled *Strike Facts.* (Courtesy of the Willie H. Casper Jr. Collection, Boyce Ditto Public Library.)

CW2 SNEED

George Robert "Bob" Snead graduated from Fort Wolters flight school in 1967. Snead was a dual-rated combat aviator and went on to serve four tours of duty in Vietnam, earning 41 air medals, including three Purple Hearts. He served for over 30 years in the US Army. (Courtesy of the National Vietnam War Museum.)

In this 1958 photograph, a bartender at Camp Wolters's newly opened Officers Club eagerly awaits the first customer. By 1969, a new four-building officers' open mess was located near the post headquarters. It boasted live entertainment on Fridays and Saturdays, 10¢ beer on Mondays, happy hour on Tuesday and Friday nights, and bingo on Wednesday nights. (Courtesy of the Willie H. Casper Jr. Collection, Boyce Ditto Public Library.)

Located on Hood Road, the Fort Wolters main library featured 15,000 volumes and over 70 current periodicals and newspapers. It had special sections for children and young adult books, and a listening room was available with 2,500 vinyl records that could also be checked out. (Courtesy of the Willie H. Casper Jr. Collection, Boyce Ditto Public Library.)

In this August 9, 1962, Camp Wolters photograph, Pvt. Arthur Davis proudly displays the metal pennant sign he attaches to his vehicle to be recognized as "Driver of the Month." Many believe employee recognition can reinforce the behaviors they want to see more often—in this case, safer driving. (Courtesy of the Willie H. Casper Jr. Collection, Boyce Ditto Public Library.)

Fort Wolters had two church buildings: the Chapel of the Flags (Protestant worship services) and Chapel on the Hill (Catholic Mass), as seen in this October 8, 1967, photograph. Six religious services were conducted at the two chapels every Sunday. (Courtesy of the Willie H. Casper Jr. Collection, Boyce Ditto Public Library.)

In this August 1967 photograph, three- to four-year-old children from Fort Wolters families are enjoying singing songs during summer vacation Bible school class in the chapel. Religious education programs, including summer Bible school, were held in the Chapel of the Flags annex. (Courtesy of the Willie H. Casper Jr. Collection, Boyce Ditto Public Library.)

The Fort Wolters Post Exchange, as seen in this 1971 photograph, offered those with access discounted prices on consumer goods and many other items. A sign near the cash register alerts shoppers to "Look for Gold Shield Items," which are discounted due to cost savings through the Army & Air Force Exchange (AAFES). (Courtesy of the Willie H. Casper Jr. Collection, Boyce Ditto Public Library.)

This 1965 outside view of the Fort Wolters Commissary highlights the size of the store. The 8,500-square-foot store was fully air-conditioned and offered over 3,000 name-brand food and household items, including an extensive selection of troop-issue merchandise. (Courtesy of the Willie H. Casper Jr. Collection, Boyce Ditto Public Library.)

The Fort Wolters Commissary, in addition to offering household goods, was stocked with a fresh supply and variety of produce and meat options. Day- and night-stocking crews continuously restocked shelves by use of a conveyor system. (Courtesy of the Willie H. Casper Jr. Collection, Boyce Ditto Public Library.)

On Armed Forces Day in 1962, Camp Wolters flight school students are seen here wearing aprons and serving a long line of attendees an outdoor barbecue lunch. Armed Forces Day was created in 1949 when US secretary of defense Louis Johnson replaced separate military branch days with a single-day celebration. (Courtesy of the Willie H. Casper Jr. Collection, Boyce Ditto Public Library.)

On October 10, 1970, Mineral Wells area partner landowners were treated to a barbecue dinner at Fort Wolters. Landowners were recruited to allow the flight school to build landing pads and improvements on their property. To show its appreciation, the Army hosted a yearly event to honor the community partners. (Courtesy of the Willie H. Casper Jr. Collection, Boyce Ditto Public Library.)

"Bozo," a Hiller OH-23 helicopter, caught the attention of these youngsters at the Camp Wolters Armed Forces Day open house on May 21, 1962. Open house and holiday events allowed family members to see up close the equipment and operations at the flight school. (Courtesy of the Willie H. Casper Jr. Collection, Boyce Ditto Public Library.)

Children from the Emmanuel Baptist Church Bible school in Weatherford pose for a photograph in front of an OH-23 Hiller helicopter during their June 11, 1959, tour of the USAPHS and Southern Airways Company facilities. Capt. Billy R. Taylor (far left) stands by ready to answer questions. (Courtesy of the National Vietnam War Museum.)

Santa arrived in an OH-23 helicopter for the Camp Wolters children's Christmas party on December 14, 1957. Sgt. Will B. Houghton of the 864th Engineer Battalion performed the duties of Santa Claus, complete with a sack of toys and reindeer jingle bells. (Courtesy of the National Vietnam War Museum.)

WOC Gilbert Mendoza of USAPHS Class 65-13WB explains helicopter controls to Rocky Mahan (left) and Gorman Ware (center), both students from Travis School in Mineral Wells. Mrs. Wendell McCrary, their teacher, escorted 27 members of her fourth-grade class to Fort Wolters to observe helicopter training. (Courtesy of the National Vietnam War Museum.)

Three Texas Christian University ROTC Cadet Queens smile for the camera while sitting in an OH-23 helicopter during their tour of Camp Wolters USAPHS facilities on December 13, 1957. From left to right are Gloria McKibbian of Fort Worth, Dixie Berry of Fort Worth, and Martha Orr of Temple. At the time this photograph was taken, McKibbian was a senior, Berry was a junior, and Orr was a sophomore at Texas Christian University. (Courtesy of the National Vietnam War Museum.)

In this photograph, 2nd Lt. David Hill explains the function of the tail rotor and boom of an OH-23 to his wife, Janice, while 2nd Lt. Harry Goetzmann and his wife, Sylvia, observe. The women were members of a July 20, 1960, tour arranged by the USAPHS for officer student wives of class 61-1A. (Courtesy of the National Vietnam War Museum.)

In this October 5, 1967, photograph, Fort Wolters kindergarten students enjoy recess on the outdoor jungle gym, while their teachers carefully supervise. The post kindergarten offered morning and afternoon classes for ages three to five years old. Rates per child were $12 a month. (Courtesy of the Willie H. Casper Jr. Collection, Boyce Ditto Public Library.)

This group from the Little Red School House kindergarten of Weatherford, with approximately 25 children and the 13 mothers who accompanied them, toured Camp Wolters on April 24, 1959. In this photograph, the children enjoy cookies and ice cream in the USAPHS mess hall. (Courtesy of the National Vietnam War Museum.)

On September 4, 1957, the WOC Wives Club toured the USAPHS mess hall. The student wives are, from left to right, Frances Snyder, Roxi Ervi, Inge Collins, June Myers, Arlene Johnson, and Wilma Powell. The mural behind the women was created by a previous graduating class. (Courtesy of the National Vietnam War Museum.)

This photograph shows a typical example of Fort Wolters officer housing in Wolters Village. In 1963, this three-bedroom, single-unit home at 421 Patrick Street was rented for $95 per month. Students attending flight school were not eligible for housing in Wolters Village. (Courtesy of the Willie H. Casper Jr. Collection, Boyce Ditto Public Library.)

This 1968 aerial photograph is of post housing at Fort Wolters, in the Wolters Village addition. Nonstudent officers and enlisted personnel were eligible to rent housing in Wolters Village. Officers could choose either a single-family residence or a duplex. Enlisted personnel were limited to either a single or double duplex unit. (Courtesy of the Willie H. Casper Jr. Collection, Boyce Ditto Public Library.)

In this 1957 training exercise, an OH-23 helicopter prepares to land transporting a litter patient to the Camp Wolters US Army Hospital landing pad. It was the first medical facility in the Army with a service designed and equipped expressly for aviation medicine This type of evacuation saved countless lives transporting the wounded during the Korean War. (Courtesy of the Willie H. Casper Jr. Collection, Boyce Ditto Public Library.)

In March 1957, Camp Wolters US Army Hospital officially opened. The 75-bed, three-story structure was designed and constructed by the Corps of Engineers, Fort Worth District, at a cost of approximately $2.2 million. The US Army renamed the facility Beach Army Hospital in July 1964. (Courtesy of the National Vietnam War Museum.)

Two unidentified senior-level Gray Ladies assist with the placement of a new Gray Lady service stripe. The two chevrons and two stripes indicate her 10 years of service. The Camp Wolters Gray Ladies were American Red Cross volunteers who served in the dependent's clinic assisting the staff nurses and corpsmen. (Courtesy of the Willie H. Casper Jr. Collection, Boyce Ditto Public Library.)

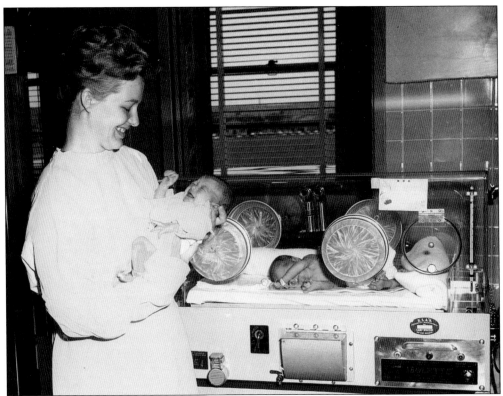

Regina Kreiner earned the distinction of being the mother of the 1,000th baby born at Camp Wolters US Army Hospital on August 4, 1962. She is holding her daughter Karen, born 999. The 1,000th baby, Kim, is shown asleep in her isolette. (Courtesy of the Willie H. Casper Jr. Collection, Boyce Ditto Public Library.)

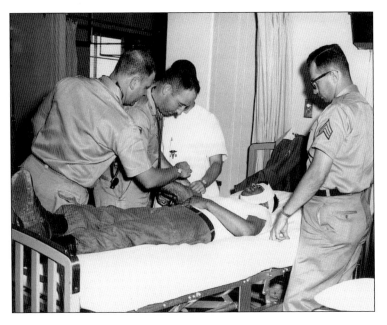

On June 7, 1962, this group of unidentified men from the US Army 114th Evacuation Hospital, Reserve Unit, practiced a mass casualty evacuation event at Camp Wolters US Army Hospital. Reserve units would often train at Camp Wolters during their two-week active duty requirement. (Courtesy of the Willie H. Casper Jr. Collection, Boyce Ditto Public Library.)

This June 1962 photograph documents a reenlistment ceremony for Sgt. Reuben Hatcher at Camp Wolters US Army Hospital. Present for the ceremony are, from left to right, Lt. Col. James Foley, Sgt. Reuben Hatcher, Col. Oliver Schantz, and 1st Lt. Dean Caram. (Courtesy of the Willie H. Casper Jr. Collection, Boyce Ditto Public Library.)

In this March 29, 1957, photograph, during the grand opening of the Camp Wolters US Army Hospital, Mineral Wells mayor C.K. Davis (left) and Col. Chester H. Meek (right), deputy post commander, pause to inspect the new iron lung machine. (Courtesy of the Willie H. Casper Jr. Collection, Boyce Ditto Public Library.)

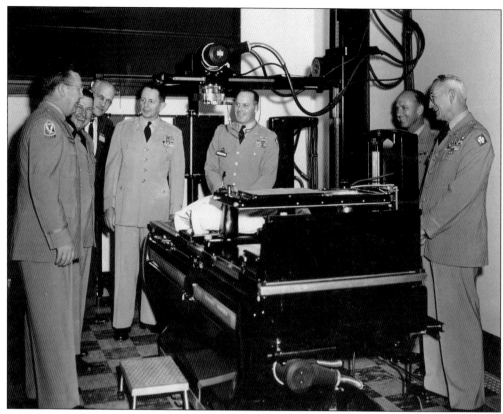

Inspecting Camp Wolters's new hospital X-ray machine are, from left to right, Col. Chester H. Meek; Col. William K. Beard, 931st Engineer Group commander; C.K. Davis, Mineral Wells mayor; Col. Wayne F. Downing, USAPHS; Col. John L. Inskeep, commanding officer; Col. Herbert D. Edger, hospital commander; and Brig. Gen. L. Holmes Ginn, Fourth US Army. (Courtesy of the Willie H. Casper Jr. Collection, Boyce Ditto Public Library.)

In this August 21, 1956, photograph, patient Donald H. Foreman of Tyler, Texas, was excited to greet two visitors while recovering at the US Army Hospital. From left to right are Texas State Farm Queen Sharon Honea of Sweeny, Texas; Maj. Ula M. Morgan, hospital registrar; and Texas State Farm Queen Patsy Smith of Lake Creek Texas. (Courtesy of the Willie H. Casper Jr. Collection, Boyce Ditto Public Library.)

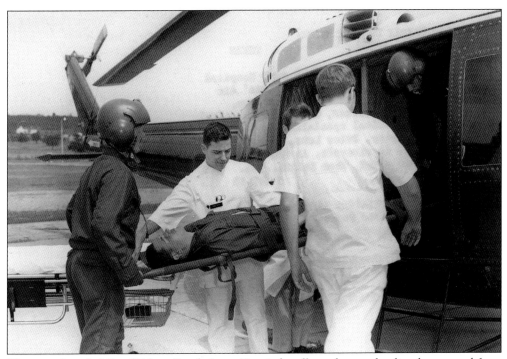

Three unidentified Fort Wolters Beach Army Hospital staff members and enlisted personnel from the Wolters Air Crash Rescue Unit place a simulated injured man still on a canvas litter into a UH-1 helicopter. On the right in the helicopter assisting is crew chief SP4 Anthony Turner of Dallas, Texas. (Courtesy of the Willie H. Casper Jr. Collection, Boyce Ditto Public Library.)

Katherine Louise Boyette was the first baby born at Fort Wolters Beach Army Hospital in 1965 to parents Ena Frances and Pvt. Wilfred L. Boyette, arriving at 10:45 a.m. on January 5. Shown in this photograph are, from left to right, the doctor who made the delivery, Capt. Donald Knaut, with Ena Boyette and newborn daughter Kathrine Boyette. (Courtesy of the National Vietnam War Museum.)

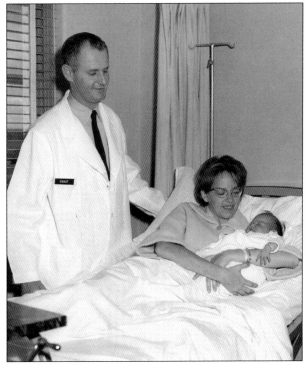

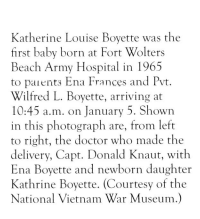

83

This group of Red Cross volunteer Gray Ladies graduated from the Beach Army Hospital program on July 8, 1964. Shown from left to right are (first row) Barbara Petty, Virginia Jennings, Doris Riley, and Barbara Mathern; (second row) chief nurse Maj. Sue Hester, Jane Phillips, Ila Redmond, Ruth Turner, Margaret Schantz, and Kathryn Evans. (Courtesy of the National Vietnam War Museum.)

In this June 19, 1963, photograph, the first group to graduate from the Fort Wolters nurse's aide course are shown with staff members of the US Army Hospital following capping ceremonies. The nurse aides assisted the full-time hospital nursing staff and physicians with overall patient health care and comfort. (Courtesy of the National Vietnam War Museum.)

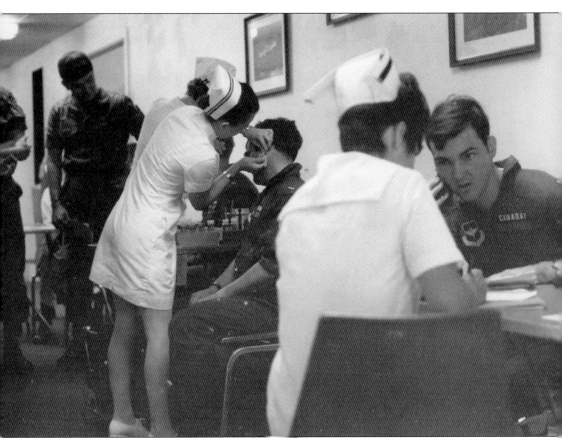

Fort Wolters registered nurses take blood samples for testing from volunteer donors during this May 1972 Red Cross blood drive conducted at the student activities building. Red Cross volunteers were staffed at both Beach Army Hospital and the Dental Clinic. Each volunteer was trained by professional medical staff on job duties specific to their assignment. Upon graduation from the job-specific training course, each volunteer received a uniform and cap, which indicated their completion of required knowledge. They were assigned according to their wishes or needs to different duty stations. Each year in August, the volunteers held a ceremony in the Chapel of Flags to honor the new volunteers with their caps and pins. These were presented to each volunteer according to years of service. The American Red Cross also maintained a field office with a resident director at Fort Wolters, which offered counseling services and help with government benefits. (Courtesy of the National Vietnam War Museum.)

In this 1960 photograph, US Army Hospital pharmacy officer 2nd Lt. Dean Carmon makes a quick exit from an OH-23 helicopter to deliver an urgent medical antidote for two-year-old patient William Dekle. Capt. William Perrin of the USAPHS piloted the helicopter on the special mission to Fort Worth to obtain the medicine. Fort Wolters maintained and kept on standby two dedicated helicopters for medical emergencies requiring a medevac. The UH-19 Chickasaw, manufactured by Sikorsky Aircraft, was capable of carrying six litters and a crew of two plus one orderly. The second helicopter on standby was the UH-1 Huey, manufactured by Bell Textron, and was the primary medevac helicopter used by the US Army during the Vietnam War. In addition to medical emergencies, a medevac helicopter was stationed at Beach Army Hospital and Dempsey Heliport during all USAPHS flying hours in the event of a possible Army flight training air crash accident. (Courtesy of the National Vietnam War Museum.)

*Six*

# VIETNAM WAR

In this 1966 view of the Bell Helicopter Textron assembly line in Fort Worth, Texas, every square foot of production floor space is being utilized to build UH-1 Huey helicopters that, once complete, were sent to Vietnam. Bell produced 75 Hueys per month. By the late 1960s, the US Army requested Bell increase production to 150 Hueys a month. (Courtesy of Heritage Room, Tarrant County College Northeast.)

JOHN WAYNE

5451 Marathon Street
Hollywood, California
August 11, 1966

Information Office
U.S. Army Primary Helicopter Center
Fort Wolters, Texas 76067

Gentlemen:

I had my ups and downs all over Vietnam with
graduates of your flight training. I found out
that they fly those things over there where
people get shot at.

Seriously, my congratulations on the work
you are doing at Helicopter Center. Without
the whirlybirds the fighting in Vietnam would
be more hellish than it is.

My compliments and best wishes.

Sincerely,

John Wayne

JW:ms

In June 1966, actor John Wayne visited South Vietnam. During his visit, he spent a large portion of his time meeting with American troops embedded in the jungle outposts, the "grunts" who faced death on a daily basis. Wayne told the publication *Stars and Stripes*, "Life is so monotonous over there that they have nothing to put in their letters." After returning from Vietnam, Wayne penned this letter of congratulation to the US Army Primary Helicopter Center acknowledging its 10th anniversary and enclosed this photograph congratulating the *Trumpet* post newspaper. Two years later, the movie *The Green Berets*, which Wayne both directed and starred in, was released in theaters on July 4, 1968. (Both, courtesy of the Willie H. Casper Jr. Collection, Boyce Ditto Public Library.)

During the late 1960s, the Fort Wolters newspaper *Trumpet* featured the column Vietnam Vignettes, which kept families and friends up to date on news stories from the war zone in Vietnam. The news shared was typically positive and at times humorous. (Courtesy of the Willie H. Casper Jr. Collection, Boyce Ditto Public Library.)

### Vietnam Vignettes

IT'S THE LUCK OF THE IRISH, according to Sp5 Bernard B. Dixon of Columbus, Ga., crew chief of the Army's "Wee Leprechaun," the luckiest helicopter in Vietnam. The chopper has been hit by enemy fire on every operation it has flown, but the rugged bird is still whirring. As proof of its bullet-stopping performances, Dixon points proudly to the 15 holes which riddle the gallant plane's body. The helicopter belongs to the 1st Air Cavalry's 229th Assault Battalion.

AS TORRENTS OF RAIN splattered on the steel planking of the airstrip at Tuy Hoa, troopers of the 101st Airborne Division's 1st Brigade and members of the Army's Vietnam Band huddled in an abandoned maintenance shed. They were awaiting the arrival of their new brigade commander, Brig. Gen. Willard Pearson. The droning rain seemed to make the time linger. Then a trumpeter tested his lip. A trombone sounded. Drummers took up a staccato beat— soon an impromptu jam session was underway. Basin Street, Broadway, and the Beatles brought hand-clapping and cheers from the damp soldiers; it was the first live band they had heard in nearly a year.

A ROARING BATTLE filled the screen of the makeshift outdoor theater at the 1st Infantry Division's 3d Brigade Headquarters near Lai Khe. The combat movie was a sort of busman's holiday for the tired fighting men—a good way to relax before turning in for the night. Suddenly the Hollywood sound effects took on new realism; the Viet Cong were adding their own ending to the film epic. The ground shook and the soldiers dived for bunkers. Within minutes, however, the enemy mortars were silenced by our howitzers and the hard-to-ruffle soldiers were asking, "What's playing tomorrow night?" (ANF)

## TEXANS AT WAR

by
THE ASSOCIATED PRESS

(Second in a series of personality profiles on Wolters' personnel released by the Associated Press.)

### MAJ James Johnston

MAJ James Johnston left his farm home near Perrin, Tex., and joined the Army to get it out of the way. That was 20 years ago.

### 320 'Huey Cobras' On Order By Army

FORT WORTH, Texas--The U.S. Army moved last week to further bolster its air strike power in Vietnam by placing a $21,795,000 order for 210 Huey Cobras, Bell Helicopter Company's new high-speed gunship.

The new contract brings to 320 the total of Huey Cobras now on order by the Army, Bell President E.J. Ducayet announced.

Bell, a division of Textron, Inc., will begin making deliveries next spring on the initial 110-ship order placed last April. The ships should be operational by summer, 1967.

This latest agreement calls for Bell to make delivery of the additional 210 ships from January to June, 1968.

The contract is administered by the U. S. Army Aviation Material Command in St. Louis. The $21,795,000 figure represents a partial-funding of the contract.

The Huey Cobra is the first helicopter designed solely as an aerial weapons platform. It has greater ordnance-carrying capability and more staying power than any currently operational ship in its classification.

Now a major and twice a Texan at war, Johnston will pass up retirement next year even though it may mean a third trip to South Vietnam.

On the wall of his den near the Army flight school where he works is one of the least fierce of fighting men's mottos: "Low, Slow and Reliable-18th Aviation Co."

"The planes that worked the Mekong Delta picked up the nickname 'Delta Airlines', and you might compare us with civilian airlines because half of our work was courier runs.

"The other half was radio relay, parachute supply drops, and before helicopter ambulances arrived in Vietnam, medical evacuation.

"We fly U1-A's, called Otters. It's a brute of an airplane, ugly and slow, but it can land on a strip of grass 800 ft. long. It doesn't climb very well, and that's when we took most of the fire on take off after making a delivery, say, out where the Green Berets were operating. I wouldn't attempt to say how many bullet holes we accumulated.

"But there was a safety feature built into the Otter kind of accidentally. They put all the gas tanks in the belly. By the time a bullet penetrated the gas tank and the floor, it was about spent.

"One bullet lodged in the heel of the boot of a Vietnamese trooper but didn't scratch him."

Both Johnston's tours in South Vietnam were with the 18th, and he was on the original roster when the transport outfit was formed in 1959. The 18th has been in South Vietnam since February of 1962 and is one of that nation's senior U.S. visitors. Johnston's son, James William, 18, began Tarleton State College at Stephenville this year and the Johnstons' daughter, Debbie, attends Lee Junior High in Mineral Wells.

The news feature column Texans at War, released by the Associated Press, appeared in the Fort Wolters *Trumpet* newspaper during the late 1960s. As seen in this column, a personal story is shared regarding Maj. James Johnston, a resident of Perrin, Texas. (Courtesy of the Willie H. Casper Jr. Collection, Boyce Ditto Public Library.)

In this photograph, six US Army UH-1 helicopters are landing or about to land in a field in Vietnam. The Vietnam War is often referred to as the "helicopter war." Vietnam lacked a developed network of roads, and the dense jungles and mountains made access to the combat zone difficult. Helicopters could transport troops and supplies quickly to remote and otherwise unreachable locations. They were also utilized for medical evacuations, commonly called "Dust

Off" missions, as well as scouting and providing air support for troops on the ground. The Bell UH-1 Iroquois, known as the "Huey," logged more than 10 million flight hours in Vietnam. A Huey is pictured on the Vietnam Helicopter Pilot and Crewmember Monument at Arlington National Cemetery in Virginia. (Courtesy of the Vietnam Center and Sam Johnson Vietnam Archive, Texas Tech University.)

After serving in Vietnam, Col. George S. Patton IV (son of Gen. George S. Patton) requested helicopter flight training at Fort Wolters. He completed flight training in September 1967 and served a third tour in Vietnam, where his helicopter was shot down three times. He was awarded the Distinguished Flying Cross for valor on the battlefield in Vietnam. (Courtesy of the Willie H. Casper Jr. Collection, Boyce Ditto Public Library.)

Gen. William C. Westmorland toured Fort Wolters on June 21, 1969. In this photograph, he is leaving for an aerial tour of the post in a TH-55 helicopter. His pilot for the tour was Frederick E. Ferguson, who one month earlier was awarded the Congressional Medal of Honor for his heroic actions in Vietnam. (Courtesy of the Willie H. Casper Jr. Collection, Boyce Ditto Public Library.)

In this 1967 photograph, Department of the Army Special Photographic Office (DASPO) photographer S.Sgt. Howard C. Breedlove captures a search and destroy operation in progress approximately 50 kilometers northeast of An Khe in the Binh Dinh Province. Members of Company A, 1st Battalion, 7th Cavalry Regiment, 3rd Brigade, 1st Cavalry Division (Airmobile) guide a UH-1D Iroquois helicopter into a landing zone during a resupply mission for the company. The hundreds of small and large battles fought in the Binh Dinh Province in 1967 inflicted heavy casualties on the North Vietnamese and Viet Cong. Approximately 8,000 enemy combatants were killed or captured. Operation Pershing was an 11-month pacification campaign beginning February 12, 1967. It was the 1st Cavalry Division's longest single operation in Vietnam, ending on January 19, 1968. (Courtesy of the Vietnam Center and Sam Johnson Vietnam Archive, Texas Tech University.)

This November 20, 1968, photograph shows a group of first wave Marines and infantrymen from the 2nd Battalion, 5th Marine Regiment disembarking from a CH-46 helicopter about eight miles southwest of Da Nang during Operation Meade River. More than 75 helicopters of the 1st Marine Aircraft Wing lifted some 3,500 Leathernecks into predesignated zones in approximately two hours. Operation Meade River was a combined search and destroy operation supporting a South Vietnamese countrywide accelerated pacification campaign known as Le Loi. The 1st Marine Division tasked its units to neutralize Communist antagonists influencing villages within a 36-square-kilometer area known as "Dodge City," which lay about 10 miles southwest of Da Nang and 8 miles inland from An Hoi within I Corps Quang Nam Province. At the time, Operation Meade River was the largest heliborne operation in Marine Corps history. (Courtesy of the Vietnam Center and Sam Johnson Vietnam Archive, Texas Tech University.)

Operation Oregon was a search and destroy mission conducted by an infantry platoon of Troop B, 1st Reconnaissance Squadron, 9th Cavalry, 1st Cavalry Division (Airmobile), three kilometers west of Duc Pho, Quang Ngai Province, Vietnam, on April 24, 1967. Members of the reconnaissance platoon are dispatched from a UH-1 helicopter hovering above the ridge line and prepare to move out in search of a suspected Viet Cong outpost. The DASPO photographer Howard C. Breedlove signed the photograph, "To My Friend Paul L. Moulton Keep Looking up, Harry Breedlove." Howard C. Breedlove served as a DASPO photographer from 1965 to 1973. Breedlove's iconic photograph of soldiers jumping out of a helicopter in Vietnam has been used on a US postage stamp as well as on the Vietnam Veterans National Medal. (Courtesy of the Vietnam Center and Sam Johnson Vietnam Archive, Texas Tech University.)

Airmobile helicopter pilots in Vietnam were in a vulnerable and dangerous position each time they were required to arrive at a pickup zone (PZ), as seen in this undated photograph of troops waiting to be picked up after a combat mission in the Long Thanh area east of Saigon, Vietnam. The assembly spot of troops in a pickup zone was often a highly visible target. The unmistakable sound of the UH-1 rotors in a remote jungle clearing would tip off the enemy on the arrival of the Hueys. In addition to being heard by the enemy, other pitfalls could spell disaster for the mission, such as mechanical problems with the helicopter or an enemy sniper near the PZ area. Pilots followed a strict ritual to ensure no troops were left behind and their fellow pilots in the extraction group were not in danger before the skids would leave the ground. (Courtesy of the Vietnam Center and Sam Johnson Vietnam Archive, Texas Tech University.)

In this undated photograph, a Sikorsky CH-54 Tarhe, also known as a Skycrane or flying insect, makes an aerial delivery of a howitzer to US troops in Vietnam. The nickname Skycrane derives from its heavy-load cargo-lifting mission. The insect nickname was given by pilots due to its unusual design. During the Vietnam War, the CH-54 was used for various missions, including recovery, rescue, infantry transport, medical supply, and armor transport operations. The helicopter is equipped with a crane in the center of the fuselage that is operated by a copilot or an engineer from the backside of the pilot's cabin. During the war, the CH-54 was one of the safest of the US Army's helicopters to fly. In comparison to the AH-1 Cobra and UH-1 Iroquois, the losses of the CH-54 helicopters were minimal. (Courtesy of the Vietnam Center and Sam Johnson Vietnam Archive, Texas Tech University.)

The 1st Cavalry Division (Airmobile) began to arrive in South Vietnam in 1965 at Qui Nhon, bringing US troop strength to more than 125,000. It was the first full US Army division deployed. It consisted of nine battalions of airmobile infantry, an air reconnaissance squadron, and six battalions of artillery. In this photograph, a UH-1 helicopter is inserting troops from Company A, 2nd Battalion, 8th Cavalry Regiment in a landing zone in Vietnam. The 1st Cavalry Division used a concept where ground maneuver elements were moved around the battlefield by helicopters. The division took part in the first major engagement between the United States and North Vietnamese forces at the Battle of the Ia Drang Valley, fought in November 1965 just two months after arriving in Vietnam. (Courtesy of the Vietnam Center and Sam Johnson Vietnam Archive, Texas Tech University.)

During the Vietnam War, the helicopter was a multipurpose aircraft. It could endure damage; take off and land in confined areas; and could be used for air assault, cargo transport, medevac, search and rescue, and electronic warfare. This qualified helicopters for numerous special missions. They played a vital role in surveillance, psychological warfare, chemical dispersion, and insertion operations. "Firefly" missions, also known as "Lightning Bug" missions, used helicopters outfitted with searchlights to illuminate enemy vehicles and boats. Once the target was identified, armed helicopters would move in to destroy them, or gunners would fire tracer ammunition to mark the target for gunships. These missions were successful in the interdiction of enemy supplies. In this 1969 photograph, a UH-1 helicopter in Vietnam is equipped with a searchlight and door gunner, ready to be dispatched on a Firefly mission. (Courtesy of the Vietnam Center and Sam Johnson Vietnam Archive, Texas Tech University.)

The UH-1B Huey helicopter variants were utilized during "People Sniffer" missions. In this photograph, pilot WO Wayne G. Hicks of the 1st Squadron, 9th Cavalry looks over a map prior to flying a People Sniffer mission at landing zone Two Bits in Vietnam. The US military used two different versions of the People Sniffer—a backpack version, the XM-2, and a helicopter-mounted version, the XM-3. The variant helicopters were equipped with airborne personnel detectors (APD), specifically the XM-3, mounted in the interior, and scoops mounted below the wings. Detection of enemy activity or concentrations was accomplished through the release of chemical effluents into the air generated by humans, such as sweat or urine. Once targets had been located by the detector, teams proceeded with an assault. (Courtesy of the Vietnam Center and Sam Johnson Vietnam Archive, Texas Tech University.)

The 91st Evacuation Hospital was located in Chu Lai, Vietnam, on a rocky bluff overlooking the South China Sea. This August 1970 photograph shows a UH-1 medevac helicopter arriving at the landing pad for the 91st Evacuation Hospital Emergency Room. In this photograph, the number 236 can be seen on the nose of the helicopter. This helicopter was assigned to the 236th Medical Detachment. The 91st Evacuation Hospital was staffed with 113 medical officers and 223 enlisted personnel. Capable of treating all acute injuries, including brain surgery as well as heart and eye surgery, the hospital treated an average of 800 patients per month in 1970–1971. A medevac ride on a helicopter was part of the Vietnam experience for far too many soldiers. Over 400 infantrymen in the 1st Battalion, 6th Infantry were medevac transported in 1970. That is a significant number, as the field operating strength of the unit was about 575. (Courtesy of the Vietnam Center and Sam Johnson Vietnam Archive, Texas Tech University.)

In this undated photograph, a UH-1 medevac "Dustoff" helicopter in Vietnam is staged ready to receive and transport a wounded soldier. A Dustoff helicopter crew consisted of four people: two pilots, a medic, and a crew chief. Usually, one pilot would fly the helicopter while the other acted as the aircraft commander. The commander would navigate and monitor all radio transmissions, talk to the unit requesting the medevac to discuss landing zone conditions and approach, decide whether or not to abort the mission, and take over flying if the pilot was injured. The medic kept the helicopter stocked with medical supplies to care for the patients. They loaded patients onto the helicopter and administered any necessary medical treatment on the way to the hospital. The crew chief kept the helicopter in working condition, performing maintenance tasks and repairs. He also helped the medic load and treat patients. Often the medic and crew chief would stay with a particular helicopter while pilots were interchangeable between helicopters. (Courtesy of the Vietnam Center and Sam Johnson Vietnam Archive, Texas Tech University.)

The decision to use helicopters as gunships during the Vietnam War led to design changes of more powerful gas turbine engines; armor plating to protect the crew; and armaments such as miniguns, rockets, and missiles. Gunships, like the UH-1 helicopters shown in this photograph, were designed to fly quickly, pack a punch, and hunt down the enemy. The most common job was providing protection for troop transport helicopters by preparing landing zones with intense fire and suppressing enemy fire. As a result of these combined missions, there was a 25 percent decrease in the death rate of ground troops and a higher number of enemies killed. All branches of the military quickly realized the gunship's potential and began using them in their operations. Soon, different kinds of gunships were created for specialized missions. (Courtesy of the Vietnam Center and Sam Johnson Vietnam Archive, Texas Tech University.)

Introduced in 1967, the Bell AH-1 Huey Cobra "Snake," as shown in this photograph at Can Tho Army Airfield in Vietnam in 1970, was designed specifically for attack. It was streamlined for maneuverability, had room for only two crew members, and could support a variety of different weapon platforms depending upon its mission: machine guns, grenade launchers, rocket launchers, launching tubes for anti-tank guided missiles, and a nose-mounted rapid-fire cannon. The fuselage of the Cobra was reduced down to a width of 36 inches, which made it extremely hard to see and even harder to hit. It was also more streamlined, which reduced drag and increased airspeed. The Cobras began seeing combat in Vietnam in 1968 and remained in the fight through 1973, with more than 1,100 of the aircraft delivered during their time in the war, although about 300 Cobras were lost throughout the conflict. (Courtesy of the Vietnam Center and Sam Johnson Vietnam Archive, Texas Tech University.)

In this 1970 photograph, a long string of Huey lift ships are preparing to insert troops into a potentially hot landing zone. The helicopters are part of the 1st Air Cavalry Division's 229th Assault Helicopter Battalion, inserting 1st Brigade Skytroopers near the Cambodian border north of Saigon. During a typical combat insertion, two gunships flanked a troop transport formation for the trip into the landing zone (LZ). Hueys carrying troops were nicknamed "slicks" because they were not cluttered with rockets or guns mounted externally. As the slicks approached, the gunships swooped down to fire rockets and machine guns into areas that might conceal enemy forces. Once prepped, troops then dropped into the LZ. Some Hueys could generate a thick cloud of smoke that could conceal the slicks and their cargo. (Courtesy of the Vietnam Center and Sam Johnson Vietnam Archive, Texas Tech University.)

Vietnam ambassador Bui Diem was the special guest speaker for the USAPHC graduation on February 27, 1970. After the election of Pres. Richard Nixon in November 1968, the United States was progressively withdrawing forces from the war in Vietnam, and the demand for helicopter pilots from Fort Wolters started to slowly decrease. (Courtesy of the National Vietnam War Museum.)

Col. Robert M. Prater and Col. Lloyd G. Huggins stand in front of the Fort Wolters sign gifted to the post by the student class 68-27, Sixth WOC Company. The escalation of the Vietnam War increased the demand for trained helicopter pilots. During the peak enrollment years of 1968 and 1969, the USAPHC was graduating 575 pilots per month. (Courtesy of the National Vietnam War Museum.)

In this photograph, Gen. William C. Westmoreland, Army chief of staff, fields questions from local news media during his June 21, 1969, visit to Fort Wolters. General Westmoreland was the US Army commander in Vietnam during the peak of the war, 1964–1968. He served as Army chief of staff from 1968 until his retirement from active service in 1972. (Courtesy of the Willie H. Casper Jr. Collection, Boyce Ditto Public Library.)

During his June 21, 1969, visit to Fort Wolters, General Westmoreland (right) toured the Dempsey Heliport. In this photograph, Wayne Schwalm (center), director of maintenance for Southern Airways of Texas, briefs General Westmoreland on contractor maintenance operations. At left is Col. Lloyd Huggins, US Army Primary Helicopter Center commander. (Courtesy of the National Vietnam War Museum.)

In this photograph, Gen. William C. Westmoreland greets Capt. Ho Boa Dinh, the Vietnamese liaison officer at the USAPHC, during the general's June 21, 1969, visit. The commanding officer of Fort Wolters hosted a luncheon honoring General Westmoreland in the officers' open mess. (Courtesy of the National Vietnam War Museum.)

Col. Leo E. Soucek assumed the duties as commander of Fort Wolters on July 26, 1971. Before arriving at Fort Wolters, Col. Soucek was commander of the 164th Combat Aviation Group in Vietnam. Soucek was succeeded by Fort Wolters last commander, Howard M. Moore, in 1972. (Courtesy of the Willie H. Casper Jr. Collection, Boyce Ditto Public Library.)

Col. Howard M. Moore assumed command of Fort Wolters on November 27, 1972. Colonel Moore came to Fort Wolters from the Pentagon where he served in the office of the Joint Chiefs of Staff. He was the last commander of the USAPHC, serving from November 1972 to January 1973. In this August 24, 1973, official letter from Colonel Moore, he congratulates the management and staff of Southern Airways of Texas. Southern Airways was a vital partner and key to the success of smooth operations at Fort Wolters for flight school instruction, aircraft maintenance, food service, and administrative departments. (Both, courtesy of the Willie H. Casper Jr. Collection, Boyce Ditto Public Library.)

DEPARTMENT OF THE ARMY
HEADQUARTERS US ARMY PRIMARY HELICOPTER CENTER/SCHOOL AND FORT WOLTERS
FORT WOLTERS, TEXAS 76067

ATZS-CO                                                          2 4 AUG 1973

SUBJECT: Letter of Appreciation

Mr. Wayne Schwalm
General Manager
Southern Airways of Texas, Inc
Fort Wolters, Texas  76067

Dear Mr. Schwalm:

1.  I would like to express my sincere personal appreciation to you and all your employees for your outstanding performance of duty from August 1956 to the present time.

2.  Southern Airways is more than a company; you have proven to be a unique group of well qualified and dedicated persons. Your judgment and diligent devotion to duty resulted in the effective accomplishment of the Primary Helicopter Training Mission here at Fort Wolters. You have demonstrated a degree of professionalism which is exceptional.  Perfection has been your standard in every task assigned.

3.  Your capabilities, initiative, and cooperation enabled us to meet the challenge of the peak period from July 1965 to July 1969, responding to the critical and rapid pace of the Vietnam buildup. The requirement placed on you to train over 1,200 Vietnamese students with the increased U. S. student load and maintain a fast growing fleet of aircraft from 195 to over 1,300 in this short period of time is only one example of your ability to get things done.  During this time you provided, and trained, an increase in employees from 529 to a maximum of 3,800 while consistently maintaining your high standards in all phases of training in the TH13 and OH23 program, and the unique new TH55 aircraft. The ingenuity of your employees in improvements and better adapting this aircraft to our needs is outstanding.

4.  Southern Airways is also an unusual organization in that you have been able to provide all ancilliary services necessary to support the flight and maintenance training, such as vehicle and ground safety, tower control, aircraft fire and crash protection,

ATZS-CO
SUBJECT:  Letter of Appreciation

refueling, radio communication and maintenance, operation of dining facilities, vehicle maintenance, training in link trainers, motor pools, supply and purchasing.  All of these functions have been "above the best".  Of special interest to other installations has been your capability to support them in the Spectrometric Oil Analysis Program, instrument program, and superior quality of painting of military aircraft.

5.  The many other ways that you and all your employees have shown dedication to performance is attested to by earning the coveted James McClellan Safety Award, Flight Safety Foundation Award, and the Daedalian Foundation Trophy for Army Aviation Safety.

6.  Again, on behalf of myself and all the military who have had the privilege of working with you, I take this opportunity to thank you for your devotion, courtesy, and for a job outstandingly well done.  Please convey my thanks to each of your employees.

HOWARD M. MOORE
Colonel, FA
Commanding

# Commandant's Farewell Message

Today the final chapter will be written in the proud history of a vital part of Army aviation training. Classes 74-07 and 74-08, the last ones, have completed their primary helicopter training at Fort Wolters and now the rotor blades are winding down. No more hover buttons, no more 180's, no more checkrides -- no more students. The stagefields, confined areas and pinnacles along the Brazos have fallen silent -- no more busy TH-55's.

However, we who have been a part of the US Army Primary Helicopter School, military and civilian alike, can be justifiably proud of our accomplishments over the past 17 years. We have excelled! Over 41,000 helicopter students have learned their primary trade at this fine school. We have a well-deserved reputation for astute and economical installation management; we have met a myriad of diverse and exciting challenges. We have been in every sense true professionals.

My congratulations to Classes 74-07 and 74-08. May your flight paths be smooth, your r.p.m. steady and your future accomplishments noteworthy.

I express my deepest appreciation to all the military and civilian personnel of Fort Wolters, including the grand employees of Southern Airways of Texas, Inc., without whose enthusiastic support the flight training program could not have been successful.

Finally, to the fine Texas citizens of this area -- farmers, ranchers, workers merchants -- Americans all -- my most sincere thanks for your wholehearted support of your Army.

It has been my pleasure to have been the Commandant of the US Army Primary Helicopter School, Fort Wolters, Texas.

HOWARD M. MOORE
Colonel, FA
Commandant

This November 15, 1973, letter from Col. Howard Moore on the official closure of Fort Wolters was published in the post newspaper, the *Trumpet*. The last graduating classes were awarded diplomas in the Fort Wolters academic building auditorium on November 15, 1973. Maj. Gen. William J. Maddox Jr., commander of the US Army Aviation Center and commandant of the US Army Aviation School at Fort Rucker, Alabama, was the graduation guest speaker. Following the graduation ceremonies, General Maddox, Colonel Moore, and C.Sgt. Maj. Willie B. White retired the school colors, and the primary flight training operations were officially moved to Fort Rucker, Alabama. The 17 years of helicopter training at Fort Wolters in Mineral Wells, Texas, ended. The formal final closing of Fort Wolters would still take two more years, to 1975. (Courtesy of the Willie H. Casper Jr. Collection, Boyce Ditto Public Library.)

*Seven*

# FORT WOLTERS AND VIETNAM WAR LEGACY

In this January 2007 photograph, Col. Willie H. Capser Jr. stands at attention on the front porch of his Mineral Wells home. The majority of the archived history of Fort Wolters exists due to the efforts of Colonel Casper securing photographs, newspapers, publications, training materials, and written history of the post, which he formally donated to the Boyce Ditto Library in Mineral Wells in April 2007. (Photograph by the author.)

Located just outside of Mineral Wells, the National Vietnam War Museum (NVWM) was established in 1999 on 12 acres fronting US Highway 180. The museum is just a few miles from the original location of the US Army Primary Helicopter Center at Fort Wolters. The NVWM is dedicated to preserving the history of the Vietnam War era and telling the unbiased story of the approximately 2.7 million servicemen and women who served in Vietnam and others who

were part of the Vietnam experience. The centerpiece of the outdoor exhibit is this UH-1D Huey helicopter, serial number 65-10068. The helicopter was purchased by the Army in August 1966 and saw three tours in Vietnam. The name of a crew chief who was killed in combat in 1966 is stenciled on the left-hand cargo door of the helicopter. (Courtesy of Jake W. Sheffield.)

UNDER THESE ROTOR BLADES
PASSED THE FINEST HELICOPTER
STUDENTS IN THE WORLD
JULY 1, 1956 - AUGUST 16, 1973

The OH-23 helicopter rotor blades shown in this photograph originally stood at the Holiday Inn Motel in Mineral Wells, Texas. A long-standing tradition of flight school students at Fort Wolters was to throw pilots into a body of water on the day they first flew a solo flight. In the initial years of the flight school, the stock tank option was most common. However, due to pilots trespassing on private property and damaging fences, the initiation was moved to a swimming pool. The 5th WOC Company, Class 67-23, Flight B-3, presented the blades to Holiday Inn manager Clarence Evans after his decision to allow Fort Wolters student pilots access to the motel swimming pool. After the closing of Fort Wolters, a sign was placed at the top of the arch proclaiming, "Under these rotor blades passed the finest helicopter pilots in the world July 1, 1956–August 16, 1973." The historical rotor blades can now be seen in the outdoor exhibit area of the National Vietnam War Museum in Mineral Wells. (Courtesy of Jake W. Sheffield.)

This half-scale replica of the Washington, DC, Vietnam Veterans Memorial Wall is in the outdoor exhibit area of the National Vietnam War Museum in Mineral Wells, Texas. The half-scale wall is the only replica wall that is updated annually so that the names match those on the wall in Washington, DC. At a computer kiosk, one can search by last name, city, or state to determine the service member's name location. The memorial wall in Washington, DC, contains more than 58,000 names. The names are listed in chronological order by date of their casualty and begin and end at the origin point, or center, of the memorial where the two walls meet. Having the names begin and end at the center is meant to form a circle completion of the war. (Courtesy of Jake W. Sheffield.)

This OH-23 Raven Helicopter is on display inside the National Vietnam War Museum in Mineral Wells, Texas. The OH-23 helicopter was the military version of the Hiller UH-12 helicopter, manufactured by the Hiller Aircraft Company of Palo Alto, California. There were over 2,000 helicopters (military and civilian) of this series produced before production ended. It was later used for the primary training of US Army helicopter pilots at Fort Wolters, where it was part of the initial training fleet of helicopters used in 1956. The OH-23 also served as an armed observation helicopter in the earlier part of the Vietnam War. The medevac version of the OH-23 carried two external skid-mounted litters or pods. The Raven could be armed with twin M37C .30-caliber machine guns on the XMI armament subsystem or twin M60C 7.62-mm machine guns on the M2 armament subsystem. (Courtesy of Jake W. Sheffield.)

The historic Fort Wolters front gate, which was constructed by flight school and post personnel in the late 1960s, can still be seen in Mineral Wells. In 1967, Col. Robert O. Lambert, Fort Wolters commander, tasked troop command to build and erect an arch over the main entrance. Construction began on the Fort Wolters main gate entrance in early 1967 to build the archway from assorted materials gathered from the post. Surplus materials were used; steel H-beams for supports, numerous lengths of channel iron, and steel mesh to cover the front. The arch was set in place with a truck-mounted crane. Workers lined up the holes in the steel plates, bolted the plates together, and declared the project a success. In 1968, two helicopters were mounted on pedestals made from the original old Camp Wolters gate. In 2010, a group of Mineral Wells citizens formed a committee to restore the gate to its original appearance in 1968. The committee continues to spearhead efforts to preserve the historic gate. (Courtesy of Jake W. Sheffield.)

During the height of the Vietnam War, the barracks used for housing the USAPHS flight students were at full capacity, including the older wooden World War II–style barracks. This group of concrete barracks in the 1960s housed WOC companies making their way through Fort Wolters's primary flight program. Although not open to the public, the barracks can be seen from Reynolds Road. (Courtesy of Derek Olson.)

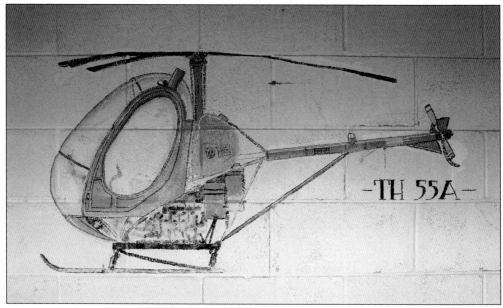

This mural of a TH-55A helicopter is an example of flight school student artwork that remains in many of the Reynolds Road WOC barracks. Student companies would often personalize their barracks with murals of helicopters. This photograph was taken during an authorized tour of the old barracks facilities. (Courtesy of Derek Olson.)

The Chapel on the Hill at Fort Wolters was built in 1941 when Camp Wolters was first activated by the US Army as an infantry replacement center. It was one of three chapels on the post and was actively used by military personnel until Fort Wolters closed in the 1970s. The historic church is still in use and can be seen from Hood Road. (Courtesy of Derek Olson.)

A monument recognizing the contributions of Southern Airways of Texas sits just inside the old main entrance gate of Fort Wolters on Washington Road. Southern Airways was a contractor providing flight training and support services to the USAPHS from 1956 until 1973. During the peak training years, more than 500 flight instructors and maintenance employees worked at Southern Airways. (Courtesy of Jake W. Sheffield.)

In 1998, the City of Mineral Wells established Fort Wolters Historical Park about a one-half mile north of the entrance to Fort Wolters at the junction of Hood Road, Lee Road, and Washington Road. The monument markers in the park have a biographical history of recipients of the Medal of Honor for those who served at either Camp Wolters or Fort Wolters. (Courtesy of Jake W. Sheffield.)

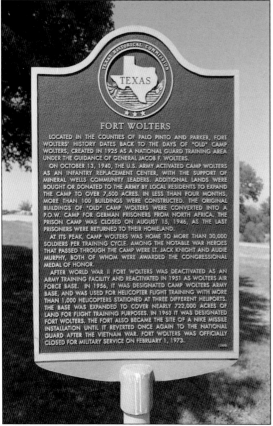

In 1999, a Texas Historical Commission marker was approved for Fort Wolters. The marker is located in Fort Wolters Historical Park, just outside of the Medal of Honor memorial. The marker documents the history of Camp Wolters and the history of Fort Wolters until the post was closed in 1973. (Courtesy of Jake W. Sheffield.)

This memorial for Medal of Honor (MOH) recipient Maj. Patrick H. "Pat" Brady is inside the Fort Wolters Historical Park. Major Brady earned the MOH on January 6, 1968, in Chu Lai, Republic of Vietnam. He was awarded the MOH on October 9, 1969. Major Brady served at Fort Wolters in 1963. (Courtesy of Jake W. Sheffield.)

This memorial for Medal of Honor recipient CWO Frederick E. Ferguson is inside the Fort Wolters Historical Park. Chief Warrant Officer Ferguson earned the MOH on January 31, 1968, in Hue, Republic of Vietnam. He was awarded the MOH on May 17, 1969. Major Ferguson served at Fort Wolters from 1966 to 1967 and 1968 to 1969. (Courtesy of Jake W. Sheffield.)

This memorial for Medal of Honor recipient Capt. Ed "Too Tall" Freeman is inside the Fort Wolters Historical Park. Captain Freeman earned the MOH on November 14, 1965, in Ia Drang Valley, Republic of Vietnam. He was awarded the MOH on July 16, 2001. Captain Freeman served at Fort Wolters from 1967 to 1968. (Courtesy of Jake W. Sheffield.)

This memorial for Medal of Honor recipient CWO Michael J. Novosel is inside the Fort Wolters Historical Park. Chief Warrant Officer Novosel earned the MOH on October 2, 1969, in Kien Tuong Province, Republic of Vietnam. He was awarded the MOH on June 15, 1971. Chief Warrant Officer Novosel served at Fort Wolters in 1964. (Courtesy of Jake W. Sheffield.)

This memorial for Medal of Honor recipient Capt. Jon E. Swanson is inside the Fort Wolters Historical Park. Captain Swanson earned the MOH on February 26, 1971, in the Kingdom of Cambodia. He was awarded the MOH on May 1, 2002. Captain Swanson served at Fort Wolters from 1965 to 1966 and 1968 to 1969. (Courtesy of Jake W. Sheffield.)

This memorial for Medal of Honor recipient Maj. Charles S. Kettles is inside the Fort Wolters Historical Park. Major Kettles earned the MOH on May 15, 1967, in Duc Pho, Republic of Vietnam. He was awarded the MOH on July 18, 2016. Major Kettles served at Fort Wolters in 1964. (Courtesy of Jake W. Sheffield.)

The Vietnam Center & Sam Johnson Vietnam Archive (VNCA) at Texas Tech University in Lubbock, Texas, is dedicated to collecting, preserving, and providing access to the history of the Vietnam War and to promoting education and a better understanding of those experiences. Created in 1989, VNCA collections contain more than 30 million pages and include military and government records, personal documents, letters and diaries, maps, films, audio recordings, uniforms, equipment, weapons, helicopters, and more. The VNCA mission is inclusive of all wartime participants, such as veterans of all the military services, government officials, nongovernmental organizations, and civilian participants active in theater and on the home front. VNCA collections also reflect the many nations involved, including the United States, Vietnam, Laos, Cambodia, and others. The photograph here represents the core supporters of the VNCA—American Vietnam veterans who served in the US Army, Navy, Air Force, and Marine Corps. (Courtesy of the Vietnam Center and Sam Johnson Vietnam Archive, Texas Tech University.)

VNCA historical collections include unique soldier experiences from the Vietnam War and project staff work closely with veterans, veteran associations, wartime participants, and other organizations to make sure an inclusive history is preserved for researchers, students, and the interested public. Examples include preserving the remarkable history of the "helicopter war" in Vietnam (top left), the important role of dog handlers (top right), the morale-boosting efforts of the Red Cross and Donut Dollies (bottom left), and the essential work of medical personnel in saving countless lives (bottom right). Augmenting the historical collections, VNCA also conducts oral history interviews with veterans and wartime participants so researchers and students can hear veterans tell their own stories in their own voices. To help make this history and the archival materials more accessible, the VNCA created the Virtual Vietnam Archive, a digital research collection that provides free online access to millions of pages of digitized materials. (Courtesy of the Vietnam Center and Sam Johnson Vietnam Archive, Texas Tech University.)

The VNCA hosts annual conferences, symposia, and other public programs, providing a range of perspectives to help better understand the complexities of the Vietnam War. Speakers include prominent American and Vietnamese officials like Amb. Bui Diem (former South Vietnamese ambassador to the United States), Amb. William Colby (former director of the Central Intelligence Agency), and Gen. Nguyen Khanh (former president of the Republic of Vietnam, top left). Additional perspectives are provided by Vietnam veterans like Medal of Honor recipients Col. Roger Donlon and CWO Louis Rocco (top right). Scholars like Dr. George Herring, professor emeritus at the University of Kentucky, provide presentations on their latest research (bottom left). While senior military leaders provide additional perspectives on the challenges of combat command like Gen. Nguyen Dinh Uoc, a commander in the People's Army of Vietnam (PAVN), and Adm. Elmo Zumwalt, commander of US Naval Forces in Vietnam. (bottom right). (Courtesy of the Vietnam Center and Sam Johnson Vietnam Archive, Texas Tech University.)

Vietnam War legacy programs at the VNCA comprise a range of activities to include preserving the history of memorialization of the war. Memorials around the United States play a vital role in helping veterans and families as they continue to grieve for their soldiers, marines, sailors, airmen, and guardsmen killed during the war. The Wall, the Three Soldiers, and the Vietnam Women's Memorial attract millions of visitors from around the world to Washington, DC, as people continue to seek answers to lingering questions about that conflict. Similar memorials have been built in state capitals and in communities throughout the United States, including the Texas Capitol Vietnam Veteran Memorial in Austin, Texas (bottom right). Additional VNCA legacy programs include assisting with United States and Vietnamese MIA remains recovery efforts, support for classroom instruction about the Vietnam War, and supporting student study abroad in Vietnam and Southeast Asia. (Courtesy of the Vietnam Center and Sam Johnson Vietnam Archive, Texas Tech University.)

# DISCOVER THOUSANDS OF LOCAL HISTORY BOOKS FEATURING MILLIONS OF VINTAGE IMAGES

Arcadia Publishing, the leading local history publisher in the United States, is committed to making history accessible and meaningful through publishing books that celebrate and preserve the heritage of America's people and places.

## Find more books like this at
## www.arcadiapublishing.com

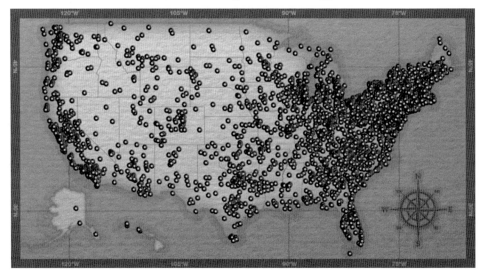

Search for your hometown history, your old stomping grounds, and even your favorite sports team.